A Flute in My Refrigerator

Celebrating a Life in Music

A Flute in My Refrigerator

Celebrating a Life in Music

HELEN SPIELMAN

SpiritSong Press • Chapel Hill, North Carolina

This book is a collection of articles published in slightly different forms between 1992 and 2010 and reprinted here by permission of the first publishers.
Permission was granted by individuals named in these articles and in email
posts. Permission also was granted by Sir James Galway for this reprinting of
his correspondence.

A portion of the profits from the sale of this book will be donated to Sigma
Alpha Iota Philanthropies, Inc., to promote music education and performance
in the U.S. and around the world.

Published in 2013 by
SpiritSong Press
320 Circle Park Place
Chapel Hill, NC 27517
www.PerformConfidently.com

ISBN-10 0615799876
ISBN-13 978-0-615-79987-2

For Fred

And did you get what you wanted from this life, even so?
   I did.
And what did you want?
   To call myself beloved, to feel myself beloved on the earth.

—*Raymond Carver*

Play from the heart; the flute is a heart song . . . like a sweet prayer, and it will teach you as well as you teach yourself.

—*Mushin Mato Wambli*

Contents

Introduction

My 13-year-old flute student, Eric, asks if he can come and use my tuner for a science project due the next day. When Eric arrives, I give him my tuner and leave him to his own devices. A short while later I get thirsty and go to the kitchen to get some juice. There on the refrigerator shelf, carefully nestled on top of a folded towel, are the three parts of Eric's flute.

Life is full of surprises—small ones, like a flute chilling among eggs and milk cartons, and large ones, like my life in music, which also began as something of an experiment and grew into two life-affirming careers. Teaching flute was the first.

I never aspired to be a musician. I am amused and amazed that I ended up becoming one. And then I began to write as a way to share my love for music. I am endlessly grateful, because these aspects of myself have brought me boundless joy, rich friendships, exciting adventures, and fabulous opportunities. Many of them are here in this collection of articles I wrote between 1992 and 2010. Reading them now, I appreciate more than ever how teaching and writing about music led me to experiences that proved to be wider and deeper than anything I had dreamed in my childhood imaginings.

I was 12 when I decided to teach blind and visually impaired children, and I never swerved from my goal. I earned my master's degree in special education, and for the next 13 years, I taught blind children who were mainstreamed in public schools. I loved my students and the work I did with them, but I became frustrated with the public school environment. Two weeks into my 14th year of teaching, I resigned. Then I spent months lying on my couch, grieving for the profession I had loved and lost. My skills had been so specialized—I thought there was nothing else I knew how to do. But a new mission was already on my horizon.

My parents had recently passed away. I lost them within a year of each other, and I became intensely interested in the field of death, dying, and bereavement. I earned my national certification in grief counseling and accepted a staff position at a hospice as Director of Bereavement Services. The work was enormously meaningful to me, but once again, I became frustrated with the work setting. The laws changed, and what we wrote in our charts mattered more than how we served our patients and families.

I'd walk around, unhappy, muttering to myself, "I could teach the flute and be happier than I am now!"

An answer popped into my head. "Well, why don't you try it?"

I had studied the flute since I was 11, and following graduate school I had played for three years in the Augusta (Georgia) Symphony Orchestra. I had even taught several students to earn some extra income back in the early days of my marriage. I had enjoyed it, so why not give it another go? I placed an ad in our town's newspaper and acquired one flute student. Then I had two. I left my hospice job when my third student arrived. Eighteen months later, my studio was strong and growing. I never again advertised—all my students found me through referrals.

Once I began teaching, my passion for all things flute and music exploded. I began to take lessons again, improving my own playing, learning new techniques to pass on to my students, and becoming increasingly aware of the wider world of the flute in the United States and internationally.

All I wanted to talk about was the flute and music—all the time.

Writing provided another avenue to express the exhilaration of all my new discoveries. I wrote about everything—the hilarious moments that happened every day, the wonder of the personal and spiritual growth I experienced. I struggled to express the rapture I found in the beauty of music—in its study, teaching, practice and performance.

In 1992 I wrote the first article of my life, "To Be Good Enough or Not to Be, That is the Question," and sent it to a small national magazine for adult amateur musicians, *Music for the Love of It*. I was surprised and delighted when my story appeared on the cover of the next issue. I decided to submit another. And then I received a phone call from Ted Rust, the publisher, asking whether I wanted to have a regular column. Me, a columnist!

I never took an English course or writing class after high school, yet my articles have been reprinted and translated all over the world.

I never earned a degree in music, yet I've been a successful professional music teacher for more than 20 years.

And now, after two decades of teaching and writing about music, I have discovered my second music-inspired career as a performance anxiety coach—a way to encourage people to heal and help them joyfully express the musical beauty they so long to share with the world. I teach musicians, speakers, actors, dancers, and business professionals to find more confidence and concentration on stage. I have given workshops in the United States, Europe, Africa and Central America and have coached individual clients at home and abroad. There was a time, three careers ago, when I thought I couldn't do anything else. And now I find a great need for performance anxiety coaching wherever I travel. Helping people free themselves from fear of performing is one of the most rewarding things I've done.

One of life's greatest surprises is that we humans are filled with more potential than we can imagine. My stories trace my own path as I followed my heart and found happiness, contentment, fulfillment, purpose, and love through my life in music. Both Eric and I have grown since we rescued that chilled flute from my refrigerator. Since then, dozens of other students and performers have shared with me—and now with you—their discoveries about music and beauty and themselves. I hope you will find moments in my stories that make you laugh and perhaps a few that make you cry. And, most of all, I hope you will find inspiration.

Helen Spielman
Chapel Hill, North Carolina

A Flute in My Refrigerator

Celebrating a Life in Music

Students and Teachers

These stories are about two sides of the same coin—learning about music as a student and as a teacher. The stories about children reveal the fragility of young people who are discovering who they are and how they want to express themselves in the world. Their desire to create musical beauty is often poignant as they cope with all the challenges of growing up. Adults, who bring a mature point of view to the study of music, often find themselves in a deep growth process as well. The fragility of the inner child remains, but as adults we discover our own great potential to learn and grow throughout our lives. I see in these stories how much my own growth as a person and my development as a musician are intricately intertwined.

A Bright Light Graduates

I t was hard to love Natalie. As a middle school–age private flute student, she never greeted me as she entered my studio, and the only answer she gave to my questions, whether "How are you?" or "Which solo would you like to play next?" was the standard of all dull teens: "I dunno." Tall, overweight, and boring, she came prepared for each lesson but had the smallest flute tone I've ever heard.

I knew that inside this person shone a light that hadn't yet been ignited. I decided that I'd address that light every time I saw Natalie, that I'd look right past the outer stuff and see the beauty in her.* At every lesson, I treated Natalie as a responsive, interesting, and worthwhile person, and poured love into her. I told her that "I dunno" was not acceptable, and sometimes I'd stand next to her patiently and encouragingly for five whole minutes until she chose her next piece.

She hated to play in recitals, so I didn't require her to, as I don't require of any of my students. She sat out a few years and eventually *voluntarily* participated. She still doesn't enjoy performing all that much, but she chooses to because she knows it's good for her, and she's gained poise and confidence.

Gradually, Natalie became less withdrawn. The first time she asked me, "How are you?" I practically fainted. A sense of humor began to emerge, and we started to laugh together at her jokes, not just mine. By the time she was halfway through high school, I couldn't stop her from talking long enough to get to her lesson material. She started telling me about her friends at school and going to the junior prom. She'd lost weight, and she looked lovely as a tall, slender young woman.

This Sunday, I had my students' recital, and I honored Natalie as a graduating senior. She played two beautiful pieces, confidently, with a lovely singing tone. I told the audience how, despite a heavy load of

*Natalie is not my student's real name; I have changed her name to protect her privacy.

3

Advanced Placement classes in one of the most difficult high schools around, she had maintained an almost perfect A average in school, volunteered at the hospital, played in her school band, and never missed a flute lesson in five years except for illness. Natalie told me once that when 8:15 P.M. came around each night, she practiced no matter what. She has the brains, grades, and work ethic to go to medical school, where she's headed after college.

It's unclear and unknown how much her flute lessons influenced the huge change in Natalie. I've heard too many teachers talk about the "losers" in their studios. One of our major international flute magazines published an article in which students were distinguished between stars and those whom a teacher would rather not teach. Teachers have spoken about students who don't inspire them. I believe they've got that backwards—it's a teacher's job to inspire students.

We are understandably fascinated with prodigies. But when we emulate those who excel, whether they're prodigies or stellar students, one of the dangers is that we may place one student above the others, and we don't see the beauty and potential in each.

My wish is that all the Natalies out there are loved, encouraged, and seen deeply by their flute teachers, no matter their personalities or how they play. Everyone has a light inside.

FLUTE List, June 6, 2008
Reprinted in *Powell Flutes E-Newsletter*, July 2008

Marisa's Goody Box

I rarely—very rarely—use my "goody box." This box, hidden in my closet, is filled with lots of little junk, none of which I've purchased. However, the few students who've actually gotten to choose something from the goody box as a reward think the items in it (plastic animals, hair barrettes, keepsake boxes, pens, costume jewelry, etc.) are "really cool stuff."

I have one girl, 13 years old, who has been digging into the goody box almost every week for about a year. This beautiful child is one of the most talented students I've ever had. I tried a variety of strategies, for a long period of time, to help her practice regularly, but none worked until we tried the goody box. Each week at her flute lesson, Marisa and I set up her weekly practice goal, and during the subsequent week, she fills in her practice assignment sheet.* If she has met her goal by her next lesson, she gets to choose something from the box. Since we started this, Marisa has met her practice goal almost every week, and she often exceeds the goals. I've never had a child need tangible reinforcement as long as she has, but my instinct has been to continue using it because of several factors in this child's life and personality.

Her mother came to me about two months ago and said, "You know, Marisa is so immature. Isn't it strange that she continues to need to earn these prizes? My husband thinks the whole thing is silly. Do you think we should make her stop using the goody box?"

I answered, "No, I don't think we should stop. It's working. With a child as sensitive and gifted as Marisa, I think whatever we can do to keep her playing and involved in the flute is what we should do. She has a deep, instinctive love for making music, and when she's ready, she'll begin to get her reinforcement from inside herself instead of from an outside source. Be patient with her. Help me teach her by doing the

*Marisa is not my student's real name; I have changed her name to protect her privacy.

things you promised you'd do: remind her to practice without nagging, and don't criticize the way she practices. If you'll do that at home, let me take care of the goody box thing in the studio."

I've been carefully and consciously helping Marisa to feel my praise of her work and to be aware of how she feels inside when she knows she's worked hard to master a certain exercise or when she's played something especially beautifully.

Marisa first came to me in her first year in middle school. She was frustrated in band class because she wasn't getting a good tone on her flute. She walked into her first lesson with a feeling of hopelessness about herself as a musician. I listened to her play and corrected several aspects of her posture and position. I showed her how to change her embouchure* to make a prettier sound, and I asked her to practice several exercises in the new book I gave her. Most importantly, I told her that she had great potential to play the flute beautifully.

I always say that I learn more about a student at the second lesson than the first, because I can see then how hard they've worked to achieve the goals I set for them. Marisa came to her second lesson with a much improved tone, and she had mastered all the exercises perfectly. By the third lesson, Marisa's attitude had completely turned around. She loved the flute and felt that she could be good at it. All she had needed was a little encouragement and guidance.

Over the next year or two, I came to realize Marisa's special talent. She developed a lovely natural vibrato and began to produce a clear, sweet flute tone. She would instinctively play pieces in the appropriate style without having to be shown, and she had very definite ideas about the structure and composition of her etudes and pieces. "I don't like the ending of this piece," she would tell me. "I think it sounds better like this." And she'd proceed to improvise an original ending that sounded equally as good as or better than the printed music. Marisa had the ability to bring me to tears at her lessons with the musicality of her interpretations.

Marisa is creative in other ways. She showed me a poem she'd written about the pollution of the earth that was astounding in its maturity. One day, I gave her a cutting of a prickly cactus I'd taken from the big plant in my breakfast room. Marisa was delighted and decided to call her baby cactus "Fluffy." A cactus named Fluffy!

---

*Embouchure refers to the shaping and application of the lips to the mouthpiece of the flute.

Last week, Marisa met her goal as usual, but at the end of the lesson, she forgot to get her prize. And I forgot to remind her.

This week, she met her goal again. I reminded her that last week she had earned a prize but that she hadn't asked for it and that I'd forgotten, too! I told her this was a sign that she was growing up, because it seemed that she was able to feel happy inside and proud of herself without needing a tangible gift.

She looked right in my eyes and said, "I know." And she put her little hand on her heart, and I knew from that gesture more than anything else that she was getting it, that she could feel in her heart the satisfaction that comes from achieving a personal goal.

Ah, Marisa, I've changed your name to protect your privacy and to allow you to continue your fragile, scary, exciting growing-up process without self-consciousness or embarrassment. But maybe, one day when you're a lot older, I might show this to you. This was a momentous day in your flute playing journey and a momentous day in your life. Thank you for letting me see your soul. I love you deeply. I want to keep walking your musical journey with you because, by letting me see your soul, I can see my own.

Marisa chose a prize for her work this week, and when I gave her the choice, she also chose one for last week. But the prize didn't matter any more. Soon, I bet that goody box will be staying in my closet, and Marisa will be looking inside herself for the prize.

Powell Flutes E-Newsletter, December 2008

A Musical Miracle

When Donna, a 44-year-old beginner, first came to me for flute lessons, she took beta-blocker drugs to subdue her extreme anxiety. She didn't share this information until a year later, after deep trust had developed between us. What she did say, that first day, was that she had been traumatized musically during her youth. She started studying piano as a college student, making a late decision to become a music major.

Donna continued, "My teachers treated me kindly but the same as the other students, who had studied for years. No one realized what it was like for me to come into it with so little knowledge. I felt I had to make up for lost time and that I was unable to live up to my professors' expectations." The sensitive person and musician inside Donna was not nurtured. Being required to play at recitals filled her with dread, and she described two such occasions when she "fell completely apart." Donna gradually had lost her love of playing; the music inside simply couldn't come out because she had become too focused on technical perfection. She eventually had dropped music as a career goal and had become a successful, respected psychiatrist instead. For the next 25 years, although she had continued to enjoy listening to music, her desire to play was stifled.

I often reflect on how even our most suppressed longings find a means of expression and how, when the student is ready, the teacher will appear. Donna found me and started to study the flute. She often showed signs of tension during lessons. Her palms would be sweaty, she'd laugh nervously, and she would mention tightness and discomfort in her hands, upper back and legs. I acknowledged her fear, let her know that I understood, and shared with her some of my own fears about performing and taking lessons. I reminded her, over and over, that the beauty of her music was not dependent on perfect playing, and that I respected her as a person and as a musician, no matter how many wrong notes she might play or how long it might take her to master a particular technique.

Donna, like many of my adult students, was hard on herself. When she miscounted a rhythm, she'd stop and say, "No!" She'd listen to James Galway's recordings and become discouraged at how "awful" she sounded compared to him. If I complimented her on a particular passage, she'd respond, "Well, it needs more work." I gently but persistently encouraged her to focus on the positive. Donna practiced her flute conscientiously, and I knew that she would keep making progress. The communication of my steadfast faith in her allowed her to know that no matter what she did musically, I would believe in her, respect her, and love her and her music.

The thought of playing in our recitals literally gave Donna nightmares. I don't require my students to play at recitals, but she did choose to attend and listen. She left the minute the last note was played, not stopping to chat and have refreshments, because it had made her too anxious simply to sit there and watch other students perform.

Gradually, this healing journey that Donna and I had undertaken began to enter more fruitful regions. She became more relaxed at lessons. Occasionally, instead of a harsh "No!" she would say, "I can do this." A new acceptance grew in Donna's heart as she dropped the notion that she had to sound like Galway to be good, and as she embraced the possibility that her music was lovely.

When Donna told me, after two years, that she wanted to participate in our Christmas recital, I rejoiced, not because that is my goal for my students—it isn't—but because that was her goal for herself. She selected a piece that was difficult for her. Although my students choose their pieces, I suggest alternates when there is a good reason not to play a particular piece. In Donna's case, I said, "You can perform this one if you like. However, because of your history, we want to program for success, and another piece would be less demanding on your breathing. What's important is that you feel good about yourself and have a satisfying experience." Donna selected a different piece. We spent months preparing her piece, working even more deeply on processing her fear of taking such a big step. Donna had asked me if she could back out at the last minute, and I had agreed. So, on the day of the recital, I wasn't sure if she'd actually show up.

But show up she did. When it was her turn, I said a special silent prayer for her. Donna played her piece beautifully, with composure, musical expression, and almost flawless technique. No one else in the room knew what an incredible struggle it had been for her to come to that point in her life. No one else knew of her courage, persistence, and determination. But I was watching and hearing a miracle, the expression of nothing less than the mystery of the human spirit.

After the recital, Donna said, "Thank you, Helen, for helping me heal 25 years of pain. I felt wonderful and free. Do you know what helped me as I performed? From the corner of my eye, I noticed your foot moving in time to the music I played. That small gesture made me feel so supported and comforted and as though you were with me all the way."

Last week Donna signed up for our spring recital.

Music for the Love of It, June 1993

Munchies, Mendelssohn, and a Masterclass

Four of my high school students arrived at my home last Sunday, ready to travel down the road with me to another flute adventure. While I took just a few minutes to gather my sunglasses and a few other last-minute items, they found it impossible to wait another second to dive into their snacks and drinks. They sat around my kitchen table munching on the candy, chips, cookies, and Cokes they'd brought along.

My husband, a health-conscious physician, observed them with great amusement. "Hmmmm, I see you brought along all of the four nutritious food groups," he remarked with a smile, "sugar, fat, salt, and caffeine." They paused long enough to stare at him blankly for sharing this irrelevant and totally boring information.

"OK, time to go!" I said. We went outside to my car, where the three girls determined that the only boy should sit up front. I wasn't paying too much attention to the negotiations, but I didn't hear much protest from him.

We took off for Winston-Salem, a drive of one and a half hours, on what was a perfect, sunny Carolina day. We were headed to the home of Dr. Tadeu Coelho, the flute professor at the North Carolina School of the Arts, who was going to give us a private masterclass. These four students, two seniors and two sophomores, had signed up, and they were excited.

As they continued munching, crunching, and slurping along the interstate, we listened to a CD of Holst's *The Planets* that one of them had brought along. After that, I popped my copy of Hungarian flutist János Bálint playing the Mendelssohn *Violin Concerto* on flute, probably the most amazing flute CD I own. The reaction in the car was a hushed "woooooow." I was struck by how enthusiastic, how deeply in love with the flute these kids are, with their hunger to learn and the true pleasure they derive from encountering glorious new facets of the flute.

Tadeu and his wife Irna welcomed us so warmly into their home that we felt immediately comfortable. My students and I loved being greeted by their two little dogs, and we were most impressed, captivated, and entertained by 8-year-old Lucas, the spitting image of his dad. Lucas was as friendly as he could be, and he set up an entire art gallery of his fine paintings for us to browse through. He was adorable, and my students are still, two weeks later, talking of him with affection.

Our class took place in Tadeu's spacious downstairs studio, where he spent a generous amount of time with each student. His ability as a teacher is phenomenal. He worked on different elements with each student, so that the class as a whole covered a wide variety of topics. For each point he touched upon, I saw the observing students trying it out on their own flutes as well. His ability to elicit positive change in tone, expressiveness, and technical ability in a short time is amazing. He uses a variety of teaching techniques and methods that are clever, unique, and highly effective. I gained so much as a player and teacher by observing him.

He showed us how he practices scales while walking on a treadmill. "It saves time," he told us. "It makes your workout harder, and it mimics how you feel when you perform while nervous and you think you have no air." He took photos of each of the students' embouchures and uploaded them to his computer. He analyzed each one in detail and compared them to embouchures of many of the great past and present flutists, all of whose embouchures he had kept on file. Fascinating! He performed for us, graciously inviting our most advanced student, Martha Long, to play in unison with him. She kept up with him . . . part of the time!

After our class, Irna and Tadeu served us pizza and cookies—how kind and thoughtful! We had time to chat and get to know each other.

It had become dark and stormy when we finally left for home. Immediately, out came the snack bags. The fact that we'd just had dinner seemed to be quite irrelevant. My heart overflowed with love for these four fabulous young adults who had just taken a masterclass with such maturity, intelligence, and good manners toward the teacher. They had shown such consideration and support for each other, and they had displayed such beautiful flute playing. I adored watching them be the teens that they still are.

The first 20 or 30 minutes of conversation were filled with exclamations of how great the class was.

"Did you hear how fast he played the *T and G*?"*

"He sure does have a gorgeous tone!"

---

*T and G refers to *17 Big Daily Finger Exercises for the Flute* by P. Taffanel and P. Gaubert.

"The things he said were so interesting."

"I never knew I could hold the flute that way before!"

"Isn't it cool how he uses technology so much in his teaching?"

"Some masterclasses are sooooooooo boring and seem to take forever, but this one flew by so fast. He was funny and entertaining and made everything seem interesting and fun!"

"I'm going to go home and try reading those note names like he showed us."

And so on . . .

Then, silence for many minutes. I didn't say a word either, and I just drove along, lost in my own thoughts, when all of a sudden, in chorus, came:

"CAN WE LISTEN TO THE MENDELSSOHN AGAIN???"

FLUTE List, March 23, 2004

Slow is Great

Cindy is a gem among my young flute students.* When I return from vacation, while the other children barely remember I was away, Cindy asks, "Where did you go? Did you have a good time?" before her foot hits the bottom step to come up to my second-floor studio. She often inquires, "What did you do today besides teach?" If I wear a new dress or hang a new painting, Cindy notices instantly. After her lesson, she passes my husband in the kitchen and asks what he's cooking. I tell her that for a 10-year-old, she is particularly aware of her surroundings and that I think that's good. "Our school teacher tells us to be observant," she says solemnly.

Cindy loves playing the flute and gets good support from her family. She keeps me well-informed about which songs in her repertoire her father likes best and which are her mother's favorites. She works hard on her music, repeating assignments many times without protest.

Cindy is a bright, enthusiastic, loving, responsive child. And, of all my students, she is by far the slowest learner. After two years of weekly lessons, she has completed only twenty pages in the first method book, while most young students are into the next book. She has learned a few solos, simpler pieces than are mastered by my 7- and 8-year-olds. During the first year, she learned only one or two new lines of music a week, and now she handles five or six. She understands the rhythms, taps her foot correctly, and remembers her fingerings (most of the time). She simply can't progress faster, but her love of the flute and her enthusiasm for making music are as deep as in anyone I've ever known.

I am the teacher and Cindy is the student, but *she* is *my* teacher, as well. She is my professor of patience, my mentor for making music *in the present moment*, my reminder that there is no race to be won, no goal to complete, no deadline to meet. She helps me slow down.

*Cindy is not my student's real name; I have changed her name to protect her privacy.

My own flute teacher encourages me to master new techniques slowly, advising me to concentrate on the evenness of my double-tonguing, on the purity of my vibrato, on the control of my fingers. W. A. Mathieu, in *The Listening Book: Discovering Your Own Music*, says, "You cannot achieve speed by speedy practice. The only way to get fast is to be deep, wide awake, and slow. When you habitually zip through your music, your ears are crystallizing in sloppiness." The instruction I most often give my students is, "Play that again, a little slower." Incorrect notes, miscounted rhythms, and poor tone quality are often cured with that one simple remedy.

Mathieu suggests, "Pray . . . for release from zealous celerity. Pray for the patience of a stonecutter. Pray to understand that speed is one of those things you have to give up—like love—before it comes flying to you through the back window."

I am praying and progressing slowly with more patience, more compassion for my difficulties, more acceptance of my limitations. Just yesterday, my teacher assigned an especially large amount for me to practice. I said, "I'd rather do one movement carefully than the whole sonata hurriedly. I'm not going anywhere, and the sonata isn't either! And, because I'm not a university student, I don't have to finish it by the end of the semester." Thank you, Cindy.

Cindy may never be an accomplished flutist, but she'll probably play until she is 90 and enjoy every minute. Her music will bring joy to her life, comfort to her heart, and peace to her soul. And that's what it's all about, anyway.

Music for the Love of It, February 1993

Snow and Ice Cream

W inter's cold and summer's heat set the scene for these students, *who warmed my heart with their dedication and their joyful music making. I first shared their stories in posts to the FLUTE List, an Internet discussion group.*

Frosty Flute Lesson

Last week we had yet another of the ice storms that seem, this year, to be especially fierce and frequent here in the central part of North Carolina. On Thursday, my house lost electrical power at around 11 A.M., and by mid-afternoon it was, shall we say, a bit nippy.

I call my students to tell them that I'd be home and glad to teach them, but if they didn't want to take a lesson with frostbitten fingers, it was OK with me. I have four scheduled, and three elect to stay warm in their own houses. Adam, though, my only boy of the day, and 15 years old at that, is determined to take his lesson.

His mother drops him off, not wishing to shiver in my waiting room where she usually sits and does needlework. Adam gets out his flute, puts his music on the stand, and looks at me expectantly.

"OK," I say, "we have a new meaning for the expression 'warm-up.' Let's hear the major scales, two octaves, up and down three times in one breath." Adam's fingers take off, but I don't know how they move so fluently in the cold. *I'm* wrapped in a wool afghan blanket and am wearing leather gloves lined with fur. "Good job, Adam," I say when he finishes. "Next week I want to hear them up and down four times in one breath." He says, "Sure, no problem," with exaggerated sarcasm, but both of us know he'll have them down pat by next Thursday.

We proceed through the lesson, ending with the Chaminade *Concer-*

*tino,** which he's chosen as his spring recital piece. I'm fascinated by his fingers, curved correctly over the keys, moving smoothly and quickly, seemingly impervious to the cold. Mine are frozen stiff.

The lesson ends. I tell Adam how happy I am that he came and how much I admire his motivation, and we hug and say good-bye.

Motivation. It's enough to warm your heart, isn't it?

FLUTE List, March 3, 2003

Ice Cream Parlor Gig

This summer, so many of my students participated in flute and music activities that I decided to invite them out for ice cream, just before school got underway, so they could share their experiences with each other. Last Sunday evening, we met at The Inside Scoop, a small place not far from the university campus at the center of town.

Each student told a little about what they did over the summer—touring Europe as principal flute of a national band, attending Jeanne Baxtresser's Summer Masterclass, going to a band camp, and so on. I was especially pleased that two of my new students joined us, and they shared as well.

I had said that they could bring flutes and play before eating, so as not to get sugar on the pads. The owner of the place was happy to allow us to play our flutes. However, no one was "in the mood." So, we got our treat: "The Kitchen Sink." Fifteen scoops of ice cream, six toppings, fudge sauce—a decadent indulgence. You get the picture.

They had no trouble scarfing it down while talking flute talk (a conversation that was *not* directed by me). Who won what competition, who plays too sharp in band class, what pieces they were going to play for recital, and so on. They were really into flutes! The exception was the youngest, who was mostly into discovering what toppings he could find at the bottom of his bowl.

Then, *after* they ate, they decided to play. Fine with me. I did ask them to go rinse their mouths with water first. Every one of them got up, right there in the noisy ice cream parlor, and played a piece of music.

They are such hams. The other customers in the shop paid us no attention, and we paid them no attention. The kids got a big kick out of it, saying they'd never played in an ice cream place before, that it was really

*Cecile Chaminade, *Concertino for Flute*, Opus 107.

"cool." We heard everything from a quarter-note rendition of Beethoven's *Ode to Joy* to the Burton *Sonatina*.*

We were there for over two hours before they called their chauffeurs (moms or dads) to pick them up. They had fun, and I did, too.

FLUTE List, August 24, 2003

*Eldin Burton, *Sonatina for Flute and Piano*.

Learning to Say No

For seven years during my adolescence, I took flute lessons from a teacher who constantly smoked cigars in his studio. I hated the odor, and it sometimes made me feel sick, but I never asked him to stop, and I didn't even mention it to my parents. The thought of changing teachers didn't occur to me although I lived in New York City, where there were many superb instructors. In college, I was so intimidated by my professors that I was unable to ask questions in class, let alone answer them.

As I continued my flute studies into young adulthood, my private teachers assigned pieces for me to study, some of which I disliked immensely. Even though the pieces meant nothing to me, I practiced them endlessly, never expressing my musical preferences.

What a wimp!

Almost three years ago, at the age of 38, I began taking flute lessons again after a decade's hiatus. With the self-assurance and assertiveness maturity has brought me, I have approached my lessons in a completely new way.

I live in a small college town now and study with Brooks de Wetter-Smith, the professor of flute at the university.* With every passing day I feel blessed and amazed that such an outstanding teacher lives and works only minutes away. This man is a top flutist who performs internationally, and he is an inspiring, supportive, patient, enthusiastic teacher. He is also wise and kind with a wonderful sense of humor. In addition to his university students, he accepts only a handful of private students, several of whom travel great distances to study with him.

Although I felt privileged to be able to have Brooks for a teacher, I soon realized that his perspective regarding my lessons differed from mine. When I began these lessons, my goals were to have fun while enjoying music, to become a better flutist, and to become a better teacher to my own students. My teacher is accustomed to preparing students for professional careers in music, and he was treating me accordingly. I

*University of North Carolina–Chapel Hill.

earn money teaching and am thus a professional musician, but I consider myself an amateur performer. I never have had the time, the desire, or the motivation to reach professional competence in music performance. I take lessons for my own pleasure. Brooks' other students need grades of A+ and letters of recommendation. I don't.

So, one day I did something that had never occurred to me in my youth. I told my teacher how I felt. I reminded him of my goals and shared with him specifically what I did and did not want to study. He listened with respect and shared his perspective, which I acknowledge is much broader than mine.

After our talk, he lightened up on me, and now I am happier with my lessons. In return, I make an effort to work on a few of the studies he suggests, as a way of saying, "I trust you. I will let you lead me; I will be flexible." On the other hand, I don't do everything he says. Ultimately my inner voice knows what is best for me. My commitment is to honor my innate wisdom, even if an expert tells me differently.

Recently, for example, Brooks suggested that I memorize some difficult scales and exercises. I despise memorizing things, but I listened carefully as he explained why this would be helpful to me. His reasons made sense. However, my goal is to be in joy with my flute, and memorizing would make me miserable, so I decided not to do it despite his sensible reasons.

It is still very difficult to say "No" to my teacher. I have tapes running in my head that say, "Respect your elders. Do what your teachers tell you. Don't talk back. Be a good girl. Follow the rules." Recently those tapes tried to run again when my teacher suggested I study a piece by a certain composer. I do not like this composer's music, so I reminded Brooks that I want to channel my limited amount of time and energy into playing music I love. I have new tapes in my head now. They say, "Remember your goal; remember joy. Your inner self knows what is right for you. It is OK to make choices. It is good and right to ask for what you need and want. You are a good flute student and worthy of respect, even if you don't do everything your teacher asks."

I am grateful that my teacher is open to processing all these complicated feelings; not every teacher would be. A few times a year, I invite him out to lunch, simply because he is a nice person and I enjoy his company. But I derive an added benefit. At these lunches we talk about music, our families, and where we went on our summer vacations. Talking as friends over a sandwich, I feel equal with him.

We sit in the non-smoking section. No cigars allowed.

Music for the Love of It, December 1992

Meeting Jimmy

For years my flute teacher talked about Jimmy. Brooks would say, "Jimmy does it this way," or "Listen to Jimmy's recording of that." After a while, I, too, thought of him as Jimmy.

When James Galway gave two concerts at Duke University in nearby Durham, Brooks and his wife had a reception at home for Galway, their longtime friend and Brooks' former teacher. So that Brooks and Mary Lou could prepare for the party, they asked my husband and me to drive Jimmy to their home. "I hope this won't put you to too much trouble," Brooks said. Trouble? Having the world's greatest flutist in my car, all to myself for 20 minutes, trouble? Was he kidding?

I was excited and thrilled. My students and friends asked what I would say to him. I didn't plan a speech or memorize a list of questions. After all, James Galway was a regular person, just like anyone else, and I wasn't expecting to feel intimidated or tongue-tied. Now, if I had to play flute in front of him, that would be another story. But I'm an extrovert and was looking forward to whatever would spring up spontaneously.

The concert included the fabulous Prokofiev *Sonata*,* the showpiece *The Carnival of Venice*, and, as encores, *The Swan* by Saint-Saëns and *Danny Boy*. Galway's technique was stunning, his tone spectacular. He made engaging and humorous comments between pieces.

Many of my students were there. Rachael and Kamna, both 11, sat with their mothers in the third row. Rachael came back to the eleventh row to inform me that she was sitting so close to James Galway that she could see his wrinkles. Great. I've been teaching her for four years to listen observantly to performers, to watch fingers and embouchure, to notice breathing and posture and tone and phrasing, and she sees wrinkles. At intermission, I had barely stood up to stretch when Kamna was at my side, her eyes round and sparkling, saying, "Wow, did you see his fingers? I never saw fingers move so fast. They're all exercised."

*Sergei Prokofiev, *Sonata for Flute and Piano in D major.*

After the concert, I made my way backstage, accompanied by my husband, my adult students, my young students Rachael, Kamna, Rachel, and Ramona, and at least a hundred other autograph seekers. When Galway opened the door, he was in his raincoat, suitcase in hand, ready to go. He took one look at the crowd and exclaimed, "Wow, look at this! OK, let's do it." He went back inside the room, sat down at a desk, and waited for the first person to approach him.

Kamna and Rachael didn't know what to do, so I encouraged them to say hello. "No, I want to wait for my mom," said one, and "You go first," said the other. So, I approached him with my hand outstretched and said, "Mr. Galway, I'm Helen Spielman, Brooks' student, and I'll be taking you to the party." He warmly shook my hand and said, "For God's sake, call me Jimmy. I want to get out of here. Let's go as soon as I get this over with."

Then, as I watched, I saw a truly gracious person patiently sign his name on programs and CD covers and greet each person in a friendly manner, even though I could sense his impatience to leave. When my 9-year-old student Rachel approached him, she had a strip of paper that had one blank music staff on it. James Galway seemed amused and asked if she was a flutist. After she answered yes, he took extra time to write out the opening two measures of the Bach *B minor Suite* in addition to his name. Rachel came and showed me her treasure. I told her, "Save this forever. It's special." She giggled and went to find her parents. Ramona handed him a program, and he asked her, too, if she was a flutist. When she nodded, he said, "Well, are you going to go home and practice?" and when Ramona simply smiled, I said, "Yes, she definitely is!" Jimmy chuckled.

I'm forever telling my husband not to drive so slowly, but for once I was glad about the lightness of his foot on the pedal. In the car, the three of us talked about Jimmy's four platinum and 17 gold flutes (all with diamonds), about publishing the music he records, about anesthesiology (my husband's profession), and about the new Liebermann *Concerto*.* Jimmy mentioned someone named "Lenny," and I realized he meant Leonard Slatkin, the conductor.

My teacher and his wife have a warm and beautiful home, and there was good food and wine at the reception with flute music in the background. Most of the guests were Brooks' college students, plus one or two private students like myself. Jimmy answered questions, made jokes, and signed more autographs. I was amazed at his energy, his willingness

*Lowell Liebermann, *Concerto for Flute and Orchestra*.

to be "on," knowing he had to get up early and play a concert in Pennsylvania the next day. I perceived him as a man with enormous fame but the graciousness to respond respectfully to comments he'd heard a million times.

The next morning I lay in bed reminiscing. Brooks had thanked me for being Jimmy's chauffeur, but I wanted to thank Brooks for giving me the privilege. Then I got up, put on my jeans, and went to meet with my pianist to rehearse a piece for church the next day. We were working on a movement from the *Fantasia for a Gentleman* by Rodrigo, transcribed for flute by my new pal. After the first run-through, my pianist turned to me in surprise and said, "You sound fantastic today! Your tone and phrasing are incredible!" For God's sake, call me Helen.

Music for the Love of It, April 1995

Opening Their Eyes
A Student Flute Trip to London

The desire arose in my heart so gradually that I can't say when it became a conscious thought. I only knew that I wanted to open my students' eyes to a larger world of flute activities than simply taking lessons, practicing at home, and playing in band class. I'd had many rich musical and flutistic experiences in London during my visits there, and I thought it might be exciting to organize a trip for my young students. I knew of no other place with as many flute opportunities in one concentrated area. "You're nuts, Helen," I told myself. But the desire kept pushing at me, stubbornly blossoming in my mind the way a flower seeks light through the crack in a concrete sidewalk.

I told my husband about my idea. "You could do it, Helen," he encouraged. I called a friend in London, flutemaker Robert Bigio, who responded, "That's a terrific idea." I sent a letter proposing the idea to my middle school and high school students. Four sets of parents agreed to send their daughters to Europe with me. And, over the next seven months, the flower came into full bloom.

Of the four students who signed up for the trip, Rachel Kiel, 14, is an advanced player. Alison Ryan, 12, Virginia Bates, 14, and Heather Whaley, 13, are at the early intermediate level. Barb Phillipson, a flutist and private teacher from Colorado, who has been a friend for years, also agreed to take the six-day trip.

Within minutes of our landing at Gatwick airport, the girls were affecting British accents and singing selections from *The Phantom of the Opera** at the top of their lungs, not caring who heard them. The first day when we bought breakfast items, the girls discovered that in a foreign country, even a trip to the supermarket is an adventure. After breakfast, we rehearsed our music and visited Westminster Abbey. The girls

---

**Phantom of the Opera*, the musical (music by Andrew Lloyd Webber, lyrics by Charles Hart and Richard Stilgoe).

popped in and out of the nooks and crannies, peered at long-deceased kings and queens, and admired the glorious architecture. We also saw where Handel, Purcell, Elgar, and Stanford are buried.

The next morning we visited flutemaker Robert Bigio's workshop. He showed us how he makes flutes and piccolos by hand, demonstrated his tools and lathes, and explained that he lets the wood cure for 10 years before crafting a flute from it. He let the girls play on his collection of rare and old flutes as he introduced them to the various key systems. Robert entertained them with his stories and jokes, and then ate lunch with us at a great Italian restaurant.

In the afternoon we went to the Theatre Museum, where we had a guided tour of the history of the theatre, followed by a make-up demonstration. The professional make-up artist chose Virginia out of the class of about twelve people, and amidst great laughter and kidding back and forth between him and my girls, turned her into a sea goddess with glittery green lips. Next we had a costume workshop where each of the girls who hadn't been made up tried on a costume: Heather became a cat with a tail, Rachel wore a pageboy's jacket, and Alison a romantic white ball gown. A special exhibit in the museum allowed visitors to manipulate puppets and life-size dolls via pulleys and magic boxes, which engrossed the girls for an hour.

In the evening, we went to the famous Church of St. Martin's-in-the-Field, where we attended a concert by candlelight. Martin Feinstein was to have played a Vivaldi flute concerto, but he decided to play a sopranino recorder instead.* The entire ensemble was excellent, and the girls loved hearing familiar pieces like Mozart's *Eine Kleine Nachtmusik* and the Pachelbel *Canon in D*. After the concert we met Martin briefly.

In the morning, we took off for the home of flutist Wissam Boustany for what the girls later said was the best masterclass they'd ever had. The pianist, Richard Shaw, was superb, and each of my students played her piece by memory. For Rachel, playing by memory is an old skill, but this was the first time the other three had performed without music. They had worked for a long time to surprise Wissam, who greatly favors playing music by heart. He stretched them to play their pieces beautifully.

"You've got to delight in every note as you're playing it," he told Heather. "If you're worried about the next note, you lose it."

He showed Rachel how to build a bigger piece with phrasing and not just attend to the details within it. In addition, he told her, "Practice

---

*In the family of recorders, the sopranino is the smallest and highest in pitch.

makes you good at practice. It doesn't make you good at concerts. To get good at concerts, you have to play concerts."

He told Virginia that she has a terrific imagination but admonished her not to get lost in it, and he encouraged her to project more across time and space. He asked Alison to sing a passage, and she courageously did, allowing Wissam to stretch her toward more expressive playing than she thought she could do. After the class, Wissam and his wife delighted the girls with a delicious cake and a glimpse of their new baby daughter.

Saturday afternoon and evening were free. "What would you like to do, girls?" The answer came in chorus: "GO TO HARRODS!"

So, off we went to the famous department store, with silly me thinking that we'd be there an hour or so. *Three* hours later, when I pried the girls away from the junior clothes and CD music racks, we left for Piccadilly Circus, squashed into a red double-decker bus. Finally, we were in the heart of the city, on a beautiful evening, with the lights, the incredible energy, throngs of people, buskers making music on every corner— London at its most exciting. The girls looked around for a couple of minutes and then spotted a Bath and Body Shop. In they went. With all of London's glory right outside the door, they spent an *hour* looking at makeup and body lotion in the same store we have on the main street of our home town! Amused to no end, Barb and I stood in the store and talked while the girls were happy as could be.

On Sunday, we went to Brighton on the train to a Flutewise Day organized by Liz Goodwin.* The girls played in a group class and met young British flutists. They were exposed for the first time to extended techniques and quarter tone flutes by Marion Garver from San Diego. Trevor Wye (a world-famous flutist and teacher) taught a masterclass that was informative and especially lively because of the humor he used to make his points. My students played *Moment Musical* by Schubert, which they'd been studying for months for this occasion. The last event was Trevor's *Flutes Fantastique*, which was as hilarious as the first time I saw it.** Later, we were invited to dinner at the home of Liz and her husband Tony, along with a few other lovely people.

On Monday morning we visited the Boosey and Hawkes (B and H) flute factory, where Buffet-Crampon flutes are made. We saw the ma-

---

*Flutewise is a British organization that encourages young children to play the flute.
**Flutes Fantastique* is a well-known show in which Trevor plays *Carnival of Venice* on more than 50 flutes.

chines and all the steps in the mass production of flutes in this huge plant, and we played some flutes at the end of the tour. Lisa Nelsen, the events coordinator for the British Flute Society and a consultant for B and H, met us there and generously took us all out to lunch.

Our last gala evening began with a delicious meal in Chinatown. The girls held their chopsticks like flutes so that I could take their photo. We talked about the trip and what each person felt had been good and what could have been better.

We then trooped over to Her Majesty's Theatre to see *The Phantom of the Opera,* meeting Chris Bain, the flutist for that production, at the stage door before the show. He was so nice that within a minute I felt as though I'd known him for years. The girls were jazzed up; they joked with him, displayed their British accents, and sang songs from *Phantom.* They were irrepressible in their joy and excitement, which he took in stride with a twinkle in his eye. He told us that he'd been playing *Phantom* for 15 years and, checking his notebook for the exact number, said that night was his 3,280th time. I asked him if he was tired of the music, and he responded that he *loves* the music.

The show was terrific, and from our first-row balcony seats we were able to see Chris in the pit as he waved to us and switched between flute and piccolo. After the show, he took us onto the stage, then to the under-stage, where all the machines and mechanical equipment are, and into the pit. He showed the girls his book and explained about passages that were difficult to play, and he pointed out the overhang above his chair on which he's written the names of all forty conductors under whom he's done the show. Finally, we went back outside so he could sign autographs for the girls. The woman who had played Christine, the lead role, was waiting for a ride. The girls talked to her and got her autograph as well. Needless to say, they were in the clouds. What a grand ending to a phenomenal trip.

The four girls got along with each other well during the entire six days. There was not one harsh word or fight among them. In fact, I affectionately thought of them as The Clump, because everywhere we went, they huddled together in a little circle of four. They clumped in the underground subway stations, talking and giggling; they clumped in the shops, peering at the merchandise, and they'd walk down the streets in a clump, sometimes arm in arm, talking, laughing, and frequently singing. They knew every word of every rock 'n' roll song I'd ever heard—and a few extra as well. I was so proud of them each time they played their flutes, and I was constantly struck by their intelligence, their consideration of others, and the beauty of their spirits.

If the girls learned, somewhere in their souls, that the hard work and time they spend each day practicing their instrument can be a ticket to a lifetime of rich experience and glorious adventure, then the trip was worthwhile. If the memories of this trip motivate them toward a stronger commitment to their flutes, then that is the best result I could wish for. It's likely that they'll remember this trip all their lives. And if they enjoy using their bath and body products too, that's just fine with me.

The Flutist Quarterly, Winter 2001

The Trill Seekers

ive years ago, I put an ad in the paper and posted flyers on bulletin boards, advertising my services as a flute teacher. I prayed that at least a few adults would find their way to my studio. Although I adore children, I wanted a varied student population so that my teaching day would be interesting and stimulating. God answered my prayers in a big way. Since that time, I have always had between 8 and 15 adults in my studio.

The children I taught would sometimes say, "Do you teach a girl named Kathy? She's in my class" or "in my Brownie troupe" or "on my soccer team." I never heard comments like that from the grownups, and I began to realize how separate they were from each other. So I started an adult flute group, which began meeting three times a year. The group has been so popular that, by the students' request, we now meet four times a year. We have an evening activity followed by time for refreshments and socializing. Becky came up with the name "The Trill Seekers," and we've been seeking trills and thrills together ever since.

My adult students were shy about playing their flutes in public, so for our initial session I invited Brooks de Wetter-Smith, the flute professor from the University of North Carolina–Chapel Hill, to give a talk about flute repertoire and play for us. "I don't know if I would have come that first time if I had to play in front of the others," Jenifer told me. "It was much easier to be introduced to the group this way."

For the second session, we played Christmas music in three-part harmony, as an ensemble, and no one had to solo. The third session became Duet Night, with the students playing duets, either with each other or with me. Gradually I coaxed them toward the fourth session, where they played solos with a piano accompanist.

Recently, when I asked the students how they have benefited from participating in our group, the theme of performance anxiety came up in everyone's response. "At first I was very nervous," said Jenifer, "but now it's fun. It was helpful to learn that other people get as nervous as

I do, those who started as adults like me and those who've played for a long time. Every time we play in front of each other, I get less nervous. It really helps."

Donna had a different perspective. "As an adult, it's hard to be less than accomplished at something. Our group validates the whole experience of being a learner. It shows me the OK-ness of being a novice."

"It's nice to have the opportunity to play in front of people other than in a recital with a whole crowd listening," Dianne explained. "This group has helped me build confidence and skill. And it's nice to play and not be laughed at. At home, my cats laugh at me, and sometimes my children do, too!"

Jill focused on the social aspect of the experience. "I like getting together with a bunch of flute players and sharing a common interest with other adults. It's rare to find a group of adult amateur musicians; it wouldn't happen by accident. It's a real plus for me to have this in my life."

Robin had similar feelings. "I enjoy getting together with other people who like to play music, otherwise I'm doing it alone. In my community concert band, we work together as a group, but this setting allows me to play as an individual and yet have somebody else to share with. And we focus purely on flute music, so it's a great medium in which to exchange information. I enjoy the talking and laughing and the fun of trying out new music."

"It's good to do something that's not work-related, something just for fun," Dianne shared. "And besides, the food's always good."

Jenifer said, "I've gotten to know the other folks in the group well. At recitals, there's no time to get to know anyone. It's so nice to have someone to talk to during the week, to go to the music store with, or to attend concerts together. Our paths wouldn't cross without this group. The other people in my life don't play the flute."

Occasionally my students get together for non-flute-related activities. As with many friendships, a common interest can lead ultimately to a broader relationship.

When I asked the group what their favorite or most memorable sessions have been, everyone said they liked the sessions we have once a year when the students get to play solos with a piano accompaniment. They enjoy hearing what the music sounds like in its entirety. "Hearing the other half of the music, instead of merely imagining it," Robin said.

"I not only like playing my own solos with a piano accompaniment," Jill explained, "but I also love to see the progress others have made."

Comments such as these show me that energies have shifted, that my students have grown and changed. After all the focus on nerves about performing, they're now telling me that their favorite sessions involve playing for others!

"For me," Jill continued, "the most memorable sessions are when Brooks gives a masterclass for us. I consider it a real opportunity to work with someone like him. What he can do with each individual student in fifteen minutes is amazing."

During one of Brooks' masterclasses, Donna was pleased that she could adjust her embouchure the way he showed her to. "I could do it!" she exclaimed. "It was exciting to learn something I hadn't thought about before."

For Dianne, the first time she heard Brooks play in my living room, where our group meets, was the most memorable moment. "I never knew a human being could make a sound as glorious as that. It was musical ecstasy."

I derive just as much benefit from these sessions as my students. My heart swells when I see my students play beautifully in a relaxed manner in front of others. I learn to be a better teacher by listening to the conversations we have during these evenings, or by watching a master teacher work with my students. My role as "the teacher" diminishes, and I become "one of the gang," just another person who loves the flute and likes to interact with friends in a meaningful way. My soul is nourished by the laughter, friendship, acceptance, and support we extend to one another.

I agree with Dianne, who said, "I like it all!" and with Donna, who said, "I appreciate the opportunity to create music for fun—to experience the simple, old-fashioned joy of making music."

When we first became "The Trill Seekers," I had no idea that the thrills we would find together would be so far-reaching and life-enhancing. In seeking a deeper relationship with music and with our instruments, we've been led toward love and joy, as well as social, emotional, and spiritual fulfillment. In the process of becoming music makers together, we're learning to express ourselves as beautiful, creative, wondrous beings.

Music for the Love of It, June 1995

Music 31

I saw that glint in my teacher's eyes, the one he always gets when he's about to challenge me to stretch my musical boundaries.

"I think it'd be helpful to you, Helen, to take a course in music theory. Not the course for non-majors—you already know that material. I'm talking about the more advanced course for music majors. Why don't you give it a try?"

The idea was ludicrous. Me, at age 46, go back to college? Nah.

After my teacher mentioned the idea, I became intrigued with the possibility that maybe I could fill in the gaps in my musical knowledge. Perhaps I could become a better flutist and teacher. Although I felt afraid and intimidated, I hoped I would be fascinated.

A few months later, on the first day of the fall semester, I found myself sitting among freshmen in Music 31: Theory for Music Majors. I hadn't attended a college class for 24 years.

I dutifully went to the student store to buy the required three books and two computer programs. Computer programs? Two of them? When I attended graduate school in 1973, no one had computers. I used a manual typewriter and carbon paper. I almost fainted when I saw my bill: $175! What do these kids do for money when they take four or five courses at a time?

That night my husband and I had a thirty-minute, in-depth discussion on what color highlighter I should use (I chose blue).

My teacher had recommended Dr. Brad Maiani, a music theory professor at the University of North Carolina–Chapel Hill—a pleasant, energetic man who surprised me by encouraging me to participate in discussions, even though I was an auditor rather than a regular student. I appreciated his sensitivity in seeing a question in my eyes before I raised my hand to ask it. His constant pacing across the front of the room made me dizzy. Funny, that never bothered me when I was younger. I got used to it in a few weeks.

The first weeks were challenging: a mix of new skills, like identifying and spelling intervals, and old skills, like constructing minor scales. I regularly handed in my homework and received an A on the first exam. After that, it was all downhill. We got into triads, seventh chords, species counterpoint, and four-part writing. Within a short time, I was completely, hopelessly lost.

I couldn't remember all the rules, and analyzing one chord took me 20 minutes (we'd have 20 or more chords to analyze at a time). Working with the bass clef drove me insane. I didn't have the time or the patience to become comfortable with that clef, and more importantly, I couldn't see the relevance all this had to my flute playing or teaching.

I felt frustrated in other ways, too, because this class wasn't set up for someone like me, an adult with a busy life and responsibilities other than school. Music 31 met on Tuesdays and Thursdays at 8:00 A.M. I didn't realize, when I signed up, that an additional lab, covering sight-singing and computerized modules for ear training and identifying chords and harmonies, was required. Students needed to spend several hours per week to master the lab work . . . several hours I didn't have. I'd rather spend extra time practicing my flute instead of figuring out the root of a second inversion E minor half-diminished seventh chord.

One Tuesday, I woke up to pouring rain outside. I rushed about, getting ready for class. An animal had strewn three large pails of soggy, wet garbage all over my driveway and yard. I hastily picked up the garbage, balancing an umbrella. Now I'd be late to class. Frantically, I drove the 15 minutes to campus, parked in the downtown lot, rushed across Chapel Hill's main street and onto campus to the music building, and ran up the stairs, my heart pounding, only to find a sign on the door: "The professor has canceled class for today. Leave your homework in the envelope below and read chapter seven for next week." The young man who'd arrived at the same time took it all in stride. "Oh, good," was his reaction. "I'm going back to sleep." I asked him how long it would take him to get to his dorm room. "Five minutes," he said. I couldn't return to sleep or be somewhere useful in five minutes.

Another day, I decided to do my lab work at 8:00 A.M. on Saturday morning, when I wouldn't have to wait in line for a computer station. The posted lab schedule said, "Open Saturdays 8:00 A.M.–6:00 P.M." After making the effort to get there so I could work for an hour before my aerobics class, I was met again by a locked door. The young man whose job it is to open the lab didn't arrive till 8:20, wasting one third of my precious lab time. (That didn't happen again, though, after my call to his supervisor.)

I called my trusted teacher and told him what was going on. I asked him to tell me again exactly how he envisioned this course would help me. He said that he'd like me to become more sensitive to the piano parts of my pieces, to hear what's going on in the accompaniment so that I could play my part with more awareness and effectiveness. "Yes, I want to be able to hear those things. I miss so much with my limited ears. But this class is not teaching me that."

I hesitated to quit because I was afraid to be seen as a failure in my beloved teacher's eyes, but after hearing about my experience, my teacher said he'd support my quitting. He encouraged me to continue the lab work at my own pace, which felt good and right to me. My friend Steve wisely told me, "It's never a failure to know what you want, and to discriminate between that and what other people want you to want."

I made an extra trip to the professor's office on campus to tell him of my decision. He was a little surprised, I think, and a little sorry to see me go. I thanked him for his kindness and said I'd recommend him to any of my friends who might want to try their hand at this advanced theory thing.

I have a blue highlighter that's hardly been used. When this article is published, I will highlight the following sentences: "Helen, you had the courage to take a new risk in your musical life. You had an open heart and willingness to spend time, money, and effort on something that might've held promise, but turned out not to. You stopped participating in an activity that wasn't useful for you. You're smart and competent and a serious flute student even though you didn't finish this course. You'll continue to develop as a musician because your soul longs to do so. You'll discover the path that's the perfect one for you."

Music for the Love of It, April 1998

Piano Reverie

I sit at the piano, staring at the long row of shiny black and white keys. I know how to find an A so that I can tune my flute. Otherwise, the piano is a mystery to me.

How can anyone play two lines of music at once, each line written on a different clef, each hand playing different rhythms and multiple notes simultaneously? How can anyone coordinate all this, and press the foot pedals, and follow a solo instrument as well? Playing the piano surely must be magic.

Tonight is the last time I'll look at a piano with such unfathomable wonder. Tomorrow, at age 46, I will take my first piano lesson. Tomorrow, my concept of "piano" will be changed forever.

I don't want to become a pianist, though, strange as that may seem. I'm taking piano so that I can become a better flutist. I took a theory class at the university, but it didn't teach me what I want to learn: to be able to hear and understand harmony and structure and progression in a piece of music, so that I can play my flute more sensitively and effectively.

Last month I went to lunch with my good friend Greg McCallum, a concert artist and the finest piano teacher in this area. I had decided to ask him to be my teacher, in spite of the fact that he has a long waiting list and doesn't take beginners, and I was fully prepared to ask someone else if he said no. We talked, as we always do, about our musical lives, and shared our experiences and plans. I waited for a lull in the conversation to ask my question. I was surprised at the emotion that welled up in me, because when I asked him, "Greg, would you teach me to play the piano?" my voice came out in a whisper.

He looked stunned and then broke out in a huge grin. "You want to learn to play the piano?" he asked incredulously, laughing with sheer surprise and delight. "Yes," I answered, telling him why and what I wanted to accomplish.

"That would be so much fun, Helen!" he exclaimed with a sparkle in his eyes. "I'd love to teach you, and I'll make an exception for you in my schedule." My heart opened to this gift of love and respect. He then launched into a description of what books we could use and how he would help me find what I was seeking. We decided on a starting date a few weeks later: January 15. Tomorrow.

As I sit here dreaming, I smugly think practicing the piano will be easy compared to the flute. I won't have to worry about taking big enough breaths. And how nice and comfortable it'll be to practice sitting down. No aching back and legs and feet. And, just think, when I'm done for the day, all I'll have to do is flip down the lid. No swabbing the inside of the instrument, no meticulously polishing the outside.

My wise, experienced, realistic inner voice interrupts the dream. I know that learning any musical instrument is a multi-dimensional challenge, and the piano will be difficult and frustrating and perplexing. But I'm eager as a child to try something new.

A memory comes to mind. When my parents first told me that I could learn to play any instrument of my choosing, I answered, "I choose the piano." To this my parents answered, in the confusing way parents do, "No." A piano was too big for the tiny New York City apartment in which we lived. I would need to consider something smaller. And so I came to play the flute, a choice that I've never for an instant regretted. I wouldn't trade the orchestral experiences I had as a young person or the countless other joys my flute has brought to my life, not for all the piano skills in the world.

The journey has come full circle. I live in a big house now, and the only "No's" in my life are the ones I impose on myself. Who knows where this next musical adventure will lead me?

I got amusing reactions from my adult flute students when I announced that I was starting piano. One of them immediately asked with a twinkle in her eye, "Are you going to practice?" Another's smug comment was, "Are you going to play in a recital? That will be a good show." She was lovingly and laughingly referring to all the many flute recitals she's played in as a beginner, where I got to watch her; now she wants to watch me play "Twinkle, Twinkle" or some such thing, sweat dripping down my forehead. (Little does she know that I'm eager to play in a recital.) Another dear adult student asked me, without blinking an eye, "Are you going to cut your fingernails?" I love my adults and they love me; I know they'll be my biggest supporters in this new quest.

My reverie over, I stare at the keys in front of me. Tentatively, I reach out my hand and use my right index finger to press an A. The note sounds. "A" represents the beginning. Tomorrow, I'll venture forth.

Music for the Love of It, June 1998

My Teacher

As a child, I spoke the words "my teacher" casually and without thought, because I had so many: homeroom teachers, science teachers, music teachers, ballet teachers, religious school teachers. Now those special words feel sensuous in my mouth and sound beautiful to my ears. I sense a tiny inner pang of envy when I hear friends say, "my guru" or "my coach," until I realize that I, too, have a special guide: my flute teacher.

> Of course, all beings are [your] teachers: a tree is a teacher of tree-ness, a baby of babyness; and there are wind, rocks, adversity, and strangers. But I am referring to loving humans who lift us over the sharp stones or, with the same hands, push us headlong and cater-wauling over the cliff.
>
> —W. A. Mathieu, *The Listening Book*

"When you are clear about what you want to learn, you will find your teacher," Mathieu says. "The two of you will meet because you are looking for each other." I first met Brooks de Wetter-Smith at a small non-musical gathering, not realizing he was a flutist until a friend mentioned it the next day. Several years later, when I decided to improve my vibrato, I called him to schedule a lesson. Naively unaware that he was an internationally recognized virtuoso and accepted private students only by audition, I blithely sauntered into his studio, enjoyed the lesson, and casually asked him to schedule another one. (I would never, ever have had the nerve to audition had I known. And I still don't fully understand what prompted him to accept me without one.)

My vibrato improved after a few more lessons, so I stopped going. During the interim, I attended a recital of his and sat in the audience, stunned. I knew in that moment that I wasn't listening to a merely good flute player; here was an extraordinary musician. A few months later, with a sharpened desire to become a better flutist, I started taking one lesson a month. That gradually became two a month . . . and then three . . . and now I get in as many lessons as I can between his and my heavy travel schedules.

Being the world's expert on what's best for me, I naturally informed Brooks that I wanted to study repertoire for the most part—and forget all those scales and exercises that I'd had to do in my youth. He kindly and patiently responded that if I played only solos I could learn to play them to the best of my ability, but that doing the exercises would advance my playing level. Gradually (I'm stubborn) I followed more and more of his suggestions, and his words have been borne out: I play significantly better than I did before his coaching. He knows much, much more than I about music and about being a musician. As my resistance has decreased, I have surrendered to his guidance, and I have come to trust him deeply.

> I am certain that my teacher knows my heart, has known it all along, and has given me exactly what I need this very morning— the right notes with the right qualities and intensities—to further my unfolding.
>
> —W. A. Mathieu, *The Musical Life*

This very morning, Brooks and I discussed my solo concert, my first ever, which I'm planning to give six months from now. Brooks fed me information about how many minutes of music to prepare, suggested factors to consider when deciding the order of the pieces, and gave me good reasons to continue my etudes rather than concentrating only on my concert repertoire. He knows what I need.

In the process of tackling the immensely difficult task of learning to play the flute, I turn to my teacher when I get lost and confused. Instead of spending hours researching how to play a particular embellishment, I can simply ask Brooks. When I can't decide which piece to perform, I can count on him for his honest opinion. After I've endlessly practiced the same blasted phrase and it still isn't smooth, I can put aside my frustration, knowing that my teacher will suggest a different approach.

So much of life requires self-reliance and autonomous responsibility. What a relief to know that, although the work of mastering the flute is mine, I don't have to figure it all out by myself.

On the other hand, I feel vulnerable in this relationship. I'm used to feeling capable and knowledgeable and, I've been told, I appear that way to others. In front of my teacher, I have to allow myself *not* to know, *not* to be able, *not* to have it all together.

If we're to endure as musicians, our desire to make music has to be stronger than our need to appear competent. Finally, for those of us who . . . make music out of a heartfelt desire, a lesson becomes a time of laying our hearts open. The emotional turmoil we go through may be disabling at times, but it is also a testament to the very real intensity and human significance of music itself.

— S. Judy, *Making Music for the Joy of It*

Whenever I notice that I'm looking for my teacher's approval more than I'm seeking a deeper musical experience, I realize that I've given too much power to him, and I take it back.

Nowhere has this been harder than during a performance. Although generally I'm free and uninhibited when I perform, I feel tense when Brooks is in the audience. The little girl in me who was overly criticized by her father cringes and tightens up and wants to run away. Instead of immersing herself in and flowing with the music, all she can hear are the mistakes and imperfections through Brooks' ears. This, I believe, is where my growing edge is right now. I'm working to free my inner musical child and overcome this fear. My father was too critical of me, but my teacher is complimentary and supportive, voicing corrections in a positive way. My fear, an old survival response, is no longer helpful or necessary.

Not long ago, I was given the gift of being shown that I'm on the road to success with this challenge. My adult students and I had a seminar about performance anxiety, during which the leader asked each of us to play a piece we had never seen before, without preparation. Brooks was there, and when it was my turn to play—even though I wasn't at all pleased with the quality of my playing—I imagined, for the first time ever, that Brooks was proud of me. Whether or not he actually was is irrelevant. A space opened in me in which the *possibility* of his pride in my playing was present. That awareness showed me that my self-esteem has indeed risen. As a musician, I am beginning to believe, truly believe, that I am worthy of pride and respect rather than criticism and dismissal.

When you have found your true teacher, don't hide. Wherever he or she lives, go there, even if you have to take an airplane or hike into the wilderness.

—W.A. Mathieu, *The Listening Book*

Sometimes I get nervous or insecure, but I tell Brooks about all these complexities. He looks directly at me as he listens, and I see understanding in his eyes. He's willing to talk at a more-than-superficial level and to share experiences regarding his own former teachers.

"My teacher"—such beautiful words, such a blessed gift. I'm aware of what an important, unique, and special role Brooks plays in my life. In conversations with friends or fellow music makers I often say, "My teacher explained it this way" or, "My teacher showed me how to so-and-so." When I instruct my own flute students, I sometimes hear Brooks' voice in my head or his words come out of my mouth as I pass on the skill to play this exquisite instrument. And by confronting my own issues with curiosity and purpose, I find the strength, support, and love that allow my spirit to shine with truthfulness and wholeness as a maker of music.

Music for the Love of It, October 1995

Fare Thee Well, Janette

As I do the dinner dishes, my tears drop into the dishwasher. During a momentary reprieve, I am grateful I can empty the dishwasher without stopping every few seconds to wipe my eyes. Then, with no warning, the tears start again.

I had planned to write about a different topic this month. But this is what's happening right now; this is real. Here is my material, right inside my broken heart. After wiping the sink, I sit down at my computer, and now the keyboard gets wet.

Janette is leaving. Janette is leaving me. I try not to have favorites but to love and treat all my students equally, but sometimes there's magic between me and one of my children. I don't create it—I simply recognize that it exists through the mysterious grace of the universe. Janette and I have magic; we adore each other. Her father has received a promotion, and on June 12, Janette's family moves to Dallas.

"I'll never find a teacher as good as you," Janette says. To her I say, "Of course you will; a big city like Dallas has wonderful flute teachers." In fact, I've already obtained a referral to a good flute teacher in Dallas for Janette. In my mind, though, I'm like a mother who knows that no one can care for her child as well as she can. My mind says, "I know Janette. I know what she needs. I know what motivates her. I know how to nurture her particular style of creativity. I know what comforts her when she 'messes up' in recital. I know, I know, I know . . ." Of course I don't believe this, but my heart feels it's the truth.

Janette is a great student, self-motivated and in love with the flute. She practices conscientiously and comes to each lesson well prepared. When she has trouble learning a new skill, she perseveres until she gets it. Even when I push her pretty hard, she stays with me. She's usually in a good mood and shares what she did in school or what activity her family is planning for the weekend. She asks me how I am, a rare question among my children. I love my quiet, shy students, too, but it's so easy to

41

connect with Janette. She's present. She's alive. Her whole being radiates with spirit.

Janette is an exquisitely beautiful 11-year-old. She has dark eyes set in a beautiful face, smooth, gorgeous brown hair, and a smile as bright as sunshine. I want to watch her grow up, to see her thin little-girl body blossom into the beautiful adolescent and young woman she will become. I want to know when she has her first boyfriend. I want to be the one to teach her vibrato and to introduce her to the Handel sonatas and to announce when she is ready for a solid silver instrument. But I only have six lessons left with her, and I can't squeeze a decade into two months.

I've had many students leave my studio. They move away, quit lessons, or decide to study a different instrument. I'm always sad to see them go, because these children matter to me. But I've never had as hard a time letting go as I'm having with Janette. I keep asking myself whether I should love them less. I know the answer. Love is not something I can make happen or prevent. Love simply is. And I wouldn't be who I am if I weren't attached deeply to my students. I give myself to everyone I care about: my husband, my friends, my own flute teacher, my special family friend, Amy. I don't want to put up a wall or even a veil. I remember a line from an old Bee Gees song: "Nobody gets too much love anymore." There's no such thing as too much love. The way the world is today, most children (and most adults, by the way) don't get enough unconditional, individual attention. I can give my students a little of that, and allowing that energy to flow is more important than teaching how to finger a high B-flat or count syncopated rhythms.

So, I'm allowing myself to grieve Janette's departure. I try not to minimize the loss, but I hear society's voices in my head: "Oh, come off it, she's just one of many—you have a long waiting list, and new students will come." The facts are true, but the emotions beneath them are not. As my friend Bo Lozoff, a spiritual teacher and author of *We're All Doing Time*, says, "Grief is just love with a bad reputation." Yes. This grief, with all its tears and sadness and pain and loss, is not wrong or unhealthy. My grief shows me my great capacity for love and makes me feel alive. Even my anger is OK. I spent a week being furious at the company Janette's dad works for (and I have no idea what company that is) for promoting and transferring him.

As I spend my last lessons with Janette and savor every precious moment, filling my eyes with her beauty and my ears with her music and my heart with her spirit, I'm reminded of the most important lesson of all: live my life every day and every moment like that, with everyone I love, with myself. Don't assume I have the future. Live now, aware and grateful.

Good-bye, Janette. Thank you for bringing your sweet gifts to me. Go on and have a good life. The pain of losing you will lessen; my tears will stop; I'll gradually let go of you, but I'll never forget you. Maybe you'll remember the half-hours we spent together for two years. I hope I've helped you love music and love yourself. I hope my resistance to your leaving won't make it harder for you. You have a difficult job ahead, starting a new life and finding new friends. Grow up well.

Would I again chance the pain of loss for only two short years of love? In a minute.

Music for the Love of It, June 1994
Reprinted in *Flutewise*, Sept.–Dec. 1997

Pathways:
Finding Your Place in Music

During my years in the music world, I have found that nearly everyone encounters some limitation or barrier. Musicians often have a hard time matching their dreams or expectations to the realities of their ability or to the opportunities available. They seek a balance between their passions and their practical need to make a living. They ask, "How can I find a way to make music that is in harmony with my true heart's desire?" A few of their voices are captured here.

Finding Your Niche

*F*inding my niche as a musician has been the most important and difficult part of my musical journey. Memorizing the minor scales into the fourth octave and acquiring a fast double tongue technique were easy compared to the challenges I encountered during my quest to find my true musical self.

The dictionary defines a niche as "a shallow recess in a wall." Imagine the ruins of an ancient building, with big stone bricks and small hollowed-out spaces. In my mind's eye I see an ancient woman stashing her corn kernels in one niche and maybe her bone sewing needles in another.

Another definition of a niche is "a position in life to which a person is well suited." Since childhood, I've loved playing the flute. I was good at it, but I never aspired to be a professional musician. From the time I was 12, I had a deep desire to teach blind children, and after earning my Master's in Special Education I taught visually impaired children for 13 years. I kept playing my flute but felt confused about making music. I didn't know where I fit in or what my niche looked like. I couldn't understand why others younger than I were so much more competent, and I often felt shame about my playing. I didn't want anyone to hear me.

One day, as if by accident—although I believe that nothing is truly an accident—I came across Stephanie Judy's book, *Making Music for the Joy of It*. That book changed my life, and I don't say that about many books. For the first time, I had a name for what I was: an amateur musician. And I learned that being an amateur wasn't a lesser form of being a professional. Being an amateur musician is something good and wonderful, a source of pride in its own right.

Our task as amateurs is not "to play music perfectly but to love it deeply," Stephanie wrote, so I started looking for my niche.

In the course of my search, I found my way to several niches. When I was first invited to take my flute to church, my lack of confidence made me hesitant. But one Sunday morning, I did perform. Although I felt tentative and fearful, my desire was awakened to play in settings where spiritual consciousness flourishes, and now my frequent solos at church satisfy my soul.

I played in various concerts around my state, and I enjoyed going to different towns, performing for strangers. But I discovered what makes my heart soar: playing for my friends, for people who know and love me, people I care about. So, I created The Chapel Hill Musicale, where music lovers gather informally. We meet at my house every couple of months. Children, amateurs, and professionals play all kinds of music in the course of an evening.

The challenge of creating larger musical events—conceiving and implementing ideas, coordinating and attending to details—intrigues me. In recent years I've produced many concerts. "Music from the Movies," for example, included four singers and musicians, props and costume changes, film clips, and, of course, popcorn for the audience.

I'm not a great flutist; many teenagers who attended the recent National Flute Association Convention play better than I.* But I do know how to teach, and 10 years ago, I took on students. I've built a successful studio where I teach up to the level of my own ability. When a student progresses to where she needs more than I can give, I send her on to someone else. I believe that those students who want what I have to offer will find their way to me.

At the same time I began teaching, I resumed study of the flute and had to find my niche as an adult student. Most of my teacher's other students are university performance majors who aspire to attend graduate school or to become orchestral players or soloists. I had to find a balance between how much I would let my teacher lead me and how much I'd create my own direction. This is still something that I work out on a regular basis. I've been with my teacher for 10 years, and he deserves a medal for putting up with me for so long!

Writing is my most recent niche. I never aspired to be a writer, but I was so excited about flute playing that I wanted to talk about it all the time. Writing became another medium. My articles are published all over the world, and I write for and help manage the FLUTE List online discussion group.

To find my niches, I had to overcome my inner critic. Because of the way I was reared, I had low self-esteem and always thought of myself as not good enough. I was afraid of making mistakes. Slowly I learned

*This article is based on a presentation I gave at the National Flute Association Convention, August 1999.

that playing without mistakes is not the goal. The goal is to be in joy. As Stephanie Judy wrote in her book, "Your own music is the child of your heart, and you are entitled to love it, not because it's good, but because it's a part of you."

Philip Sudo, in *Zen Guitar*, advises, "The path . . . is not through becoming the best player, but the best person."

All the parts of my life, including music, are deeply intertwined. When I function on a higher level in my relationships, or when I deepen my spirituality, my music becomes better. When I work hard at improving my playing, I relate to people in a new way and am more connected spiritually. As flutist Robert Dick recently wrote on the FLUTE List: "Dig the music, dig into the music, and dig into yourself doing it."*

Skill is less important than honesty, integrity, and conviction. These elements of living make vital music and have nothing to do with talent. When you see a child playing with deep earnestness, don't you hear the beauty in that, even if his skill level isn't mature? The same is true for adults; the truth within the heart of the music shines through when the musician plays sincerely.

I constantly work on deepening my gratitude, knowing that being grateful is one of the most important things to do in life. I could so easily feel bad because I can't play as well as a famous flutist I hear on a CD. But I can just as easily think about the average person on the street, who can't play a musical instrument at all, and be grateful for the gift of ability! When a friend asks me to play at her wedding, I can give her music as a gift. When a neighbor is sick, I can run across the street and play comforting songs.

Remember that wall filled with many niches? Claim one—or several—for your own. If the niche you want isn't available, you can create it.

People often say that I've done a good service for the community by hosting the musicales. I'm happy to serve the community, but truthfully, I started them for myself. I wanted a performance venue, and I created it.

Other people have found different niches. One of my adult students loves chamber music. Although she's a full-time physician and mother of two teenagers, she finds time to play in groups several evenings a week. Some folks want to play alone on the beach, just for the seagulls. Others enjoy performing for senior citizens in retirement communities or coaching children in schools. Many find joy in a flute choir or a village band or orchestra. Myriad niches exist for those who make music.

*Robert Dick is a composer, improviser, author, international masterclass teacher, and inventor of new types of flutes.

Ask yourself these questions: Why are you making music? What really makes your soul sing with joy? And, most importantly, what would you do if you knew you couldn't fail?

For an amateur, there is no failure. Just do what you love. Think about amateur tennis players. They reserve a court, knock around a few balls, and keep score. Someone wins, someone loses, and they all leave feeling great. They don't have the same form as the players at Wimbledon, nor do they achieve the same ball speed or score. They play because they enjoy it. And that's how it can be for amateur musicians.

With the emphasis on giving, there is no need for fear. Imagine that a friend makes you a beautiful piece of pottery, although the sides are a little lopsided and the glaze isn't quite even. Wouldn't you receive that pot and cherish it within the context of the love in which it was made and given?

That's how people will receive your music if you give it with love.

I implore you not to go near the land of "Should." Don't think about what your parents want you to do or what your teacher thinks you should do. Don't imagine how you should play as compared with someone else.

Exposing your heart can be scary, but it's human. Trust your heart, because that is where your power is.

Claim your musicality. Empower yourself to use your music to radiate love and caring. The world is in serious trouble, and music has the power to transcend our differences and create vibrations of change. You have the power to make that happen.

I ask you not to underestimate that power or the beauty of your playing. You may be sitting in one little niche in a huge wall, but if it's your special niche, the one to which you're well suited, you can light up the whole world.

The Flutist Quarterly, Winter 2000

The Music Road Less Traveled:
Alternative Careers for Flutists

When young flutists look to their future, they often envision a wonderful, traditional career: winning a coveted orchestral position or teaching at a prestigious academic institution. While these paths are possible and fulfilling for some, less traditional but equally exciting lifework beckons others. In this article, five flutists—from a Grammy Award winner to an adult beginner—share their stories and advice on forging innovative, unique professional careers.

RHONDA LARSON

"I started out with the myopic belief that classical music was the only real or legitimate music out there," Rhonda Larson remembers. "I was immersed in becoming a classical flute soloist. But deep in my heart, I wanted to make music that might be more inclusive, music for the 'wider public' that might have a larger impact. I wanted to offer something positive and to be relevant to the time I was living in. I wanted my music to serve on the level of the soul."

Today, Larson travels the world as a renowned soloist and teacher, performing her own music. She says it is a life she found through the serendipitous and timely acquaintance of many people who guided her, as well as through the evolution of quiet inner thoughts. She carried these thoughts for years because she didn't know how to change her classical music life.

A month before her graduation from the University of Idaho, the Paul Winter Consort performed there.* At a workshop, Winter noticed Larson and invited her to meet him a week later when they were both planning to be in New York. Inside the magnificent Cathedral of St. John the Divine, Winter simply said to her, "Just start playing."

*Paul Winter Consort mixes elements of jazz, classical, and world music, with emphasis on sounds of nature.

Larson explained, "I knew he wasn't asking to hear my latest Paganini. He was saying, 'Make something up.' To a classical musician, those can be paralyzing words, but for the first time in my life, I created some kind of music that I had no idea existed inside of me. Something larger took over."

Larson joined the Paul Winter Consort and toured internationally for seven years. She was exposed to traditional village music from Russia, Africa, and Brazil. Using "seeds" from classical repertoire to develop her own pieces, she began composing music and created the first of her two solo CDs. She also acquired her first ethnic flute, which remains a strong passion today.

"My path is 'following my heart,' and I have no doubt that it is available to any flutist who wishes to say 'yes' to this same inner listening of what to follow, musically. 'Following my heart' means paying close attention to what I am moved by in music.

"Be technically ready for anything," she advises. "Pay attention to what music you really, honestly like, and how you would like it to be for your audience. Act with courage even though fears are present. Say 'yes' every time something challenging comes along, as much as you can. You never know where it might lead you. Sometimes you will only get the smallest hint of a clue as to your next step.

"I am clear in my desire to live a full, real life first, with music as the path to do so. I'm not interested in fame; I'm interested in *effectiveness*. I want my music to serve people and contribute to humankind in some positive way—music is that big for me. I want to give something back that is *real* to the human heart."

DON BAILEY

Don Bailey, a freelance musician based in New York City, has achieved the perfect balance to which so many musicians aspire. He enjoys two careers—one as a flutist, the other as a software training consultant for international law firms. The financial security of the consulting allows him to be selective in his music pursuits, which keeps his passion for music alive. He's not sure whether he chose an alternative career or whether it simply evolved.

In college, Bailey says he was naive about what a life in music meant, so he double-majored in music and psychology and spent seven years as a vocational counselor for hearing-impaired job seekers. At age 27, he missed music and entered graduate school, studying flute at the University of North Texas, then at Aspen and in France with Albert Tipton and Alain Marion. After beginning a professional career in Dallas with the Dallas Chamber and Bach Orchestras, he later taught at a small Louisiana university where he lacked inspiration and his interest withered. In 1992, Bailey moved to New York City to freelance. To pay the bills, he took a temp job in a law firm and still works as a software consultant, often remotely via the Internet, but only as a means to an end. "My flute comes first," he says.

"I never believed that I was a non-flutist," says Bailey. "I played on cruise ships and produced my own recordings. Now I tour with my favorite pianists and attend festivals, most recently the Spoleto Festival in Italy, where I performed with the resident string quartet and organized the chamber music concerts. I recently recorded one of Gian Carlo Menotti's operas with principal players from The Dallas Symphony and Opera Orchestras.

"I follow my instincts and prepare for the consequences. It's hard in the arts." Bailey advises flutists to stay in shape because we are only as good as our last performance. A professional, friendly attitude is imperative, he says. "Be proactive by creating your own tours, recordings, and recitals."

Bailey intends to do more tours and recordings. He can't promise he'll stay put. "I need to be stimulated and inspired. I am a restless spirit."

LEA PEARSON

"I once heard Kathy Borst Jones say to her students, 'Follow your interests and get really good at one thing.'* That's what I've done," Lea Pearson says. "I never intended to be a professional musician. I saw my family play boring gigs, so I went into mental health and education, but I couldn't live without music."

Pearson went back to grad school to study flute, and a traditional orchestral job followed. She also taught itinerantly and became involved in many arts education programs.

"Something was wrong because I was always playing with pain. At age 45, I decided to either learn how to use my body better or stop playing." Pearson studied Alexander Technique with Barbara Conable, the founder of Andover Educators, and was among the first group of musicians officially trained to teach Body Mapping.** Leaving her family for

*Katherine Borst Jones is professor of flute at The Ohio State University.
**Body Mapping is the process of correcting and revising the brain maps that control movement to help musicians move freely, improve performance, and prevent injury. Alexander Technique also re-educates mind and body to improve performance and prevent injury.

six months, she fulfilled a 12-year goal to study with Liisa Ruoho in Finland.* The thesis Pearson wrote to earn her degree became the basis for her book about Body Mapping and flute playing.

"It's only been in the past two years that I have finally found work that pulls together all my strengths and abilities—helping musicians understand and use their bodies healthfully. With this clarity and passion that I'm doing the right thing for me, I try to balance what's most effective, because I can't do everything. In my heart, I've always identified myself as a musician, even when I've had other identities."

Pearson's career partly found her, she says. Body Mapping was what she needed to support her own musicianship, and it is what she feels she was born to do.

"I love to empower people to make their own changes—to make the musical choices they want because they have access to their whole mind/body.

"Life is a series of choices and compromises. When you want to be a musician, *and* have relationships, *and* perform *and* teach, you're constantly faced with the need for patience. Which one will I do now? No one else can tell you what you should do, when. Music is one part of who you are, but it's not all of who you are. Our music schools put people into molds. If you want something that's different, structure your life to get it.

"Stay open," Pearson advises, "and use your senses to be alert, alive, and awake to the present. That's how we're designed to work."

JIM LASOTA

Jim Lasota always wanted to play the flute but couldn't because there was a clarinet in the closet. The first thing he did after high school was buy a used flute and teach himself to play. When someone in the arts community panicked because a flutist canceled out of a job at the last minute, Lasota got a call to sub in a musical theater. It was the first step to his current work as an orchestral contractor and performer. This was exactly what he wanted to do.

"I moved to Los Angeles because of music," Lasota says. "I was determined that I could work a conventional job and do music, too. I got a position with AT&T and still have it 26 years later."

To find opportunities to play flute, Lasota started dialing churches from the phone book. He was excited about the "no" responses because each one, he knew, would get him closer to a "yes." He got playing jobs at

*Liisa Ruoho is professor of flute at Sibelius Academy in Helsinki.

several churches, got a teacher, and made a million calls until he received his first yes—and "I was right there sliding in," he says. "Since then I've had my calendar filled a year in advance, with three to four musical theater companies, as principal flute with a wonderful Los Angeles Chamber Orchestra series, and church and solo recital gigs."

Once, Lasota took a flute lesson from Carol Wincenc.* She told him, "People who graduate from Eastman and Juilliard can't find as much work as you have." In fact, Lasota gave this interview from his car, driving to a gig on the freeways in LA.

"When people say, 'think out of the box,' I say, is there a box? I'm motivated by challenges like 'no you can't' and 'that's not the way it works' and 'it's not normal.' The bottom line is how you play."

Lasota's strength in computers, and his analytical and organizational skills, led him to become an orchestral contractor. When he travels, he can conduct his contract business from anywhere in the world.

"I have many people to hire. I have top notch players who behave miserably. Others cannot wait to show up and take out their instruments. On the musicianship scale, I'd rather have a positive person who plays a '9' than someone who plays a '10' and has an attitude. We get paid for having fun. Personality is a big factor."

Lasota believes a plethora of music work is available—you just have to find where you fit in. He says being thick-skinned and tenacious are helpful traits. "Perfect players don't exist, and there's room for a thousand good players. Always be your own teacher; there's always room to get better. Study math and science, which are so vital in music.

"By going through the back door, I've been a featured soloist with orchestras in Europe. You have to be flexible and look at all the options."

KAREN BOGARDUS

"In my heart, New York City was always where I wanted to be. Something about it felt right, but it was hard in the beginning," Karen Bogardus remembers. "I temped in an office for five months and practiced evenings. It was scary, with tons of great players in the city, and I had to figure out how to make a living and still be a flutist."

Her nontraditional path led her to a successful freelance music career. Bogardus earned her master's at Northwestern and began a D.M.A.** at the University of North Texas that she didn't complete because she be-

*Carol Wincenc is a flute soloist, a recording artist, and a professor of flute at The Juilliard School and SUNY-Stony Brook.
**Doctor of Musical Arts.

came principal flute in an orchestra in Mexico. After playing principal in most of Mexico's major orchestras, Bogardus went to New York. "I hardly knew anyone in the city. I finally hooked up with one wedding contractor and then met other freelancing musicians. I started getting more work and did my New York debut at Weill Hall."

Now Bogardus' calendar is full, playing in regional orchestras, in operas, and for Broadway musicals. She regularly plays in *Wicked** and *Les Misérables*** and has toured with *The Phantom of the Opera*. Bogardus records for films, PBS, Nickelodeon, and pop CDs.

"I visualize the kind of job I want, and I believe that when I put that energy out in the universe, it comes back to me." Bogardus plays principal, second, piccolo, alto, bass, penny whistle, and recorders. "There's a big difference in these roles," she says. "It's not just about playing the flute—it's about wearing different hats. Playing in an orchestra is different than playing on Broadway. You have to adapt.

"Having people skills and work ethics is more important than how well you play. I try to have fun and make playing enjoyable for my colleagues. Being a team player, having a positive attitude, and being reliable are extremely important.

"New York is a pretty easy place to get enough work to stay busy. I encourage anyone to have a career as a flutist in the U.S. You may not have exactly the same opportunities I do, but you can be a flutist."

The Flutist Quarterly, Fall 2007

**Wicked*, the musical (music and lyrics by Stephen Schwartz and Winnie Holzman).
***Les Misérables*, the musical (music and lyrics by Claude-Michel Schönberg and Alain Boublil).

Polishing the Jewels:
Reflections of an Amateur Flutist

I've always loved studying music and the flute, but I never wanted to be a professional musician. Another ambition burned in my young soul, a fire I followed to gratifying work in special education and bereavement counseling.

At 39, I left those careers behind and began teaching flute full-time. I earn money teaching, so I could be considered a professional, but I happily consider myself an amateur flutist. I don't have a degree in music, and I haven't reached a level of professional competence on my instrument. I perform often, but hardly ever for money. I continue to take flute lessons and practice regularly, but I don't kill myself doing it. I have no particular goal, such as admission to a conservatory or an orchestra position. I simply want to become a better musician, at whatever pace that happens, and enjoy the music and the learning process in a non-stressful way.

The word "amateur" has its roots in the Latin word "amator" (lover). I play because I love to play, not because I have to.

"Love is the most important quality to bring to any task. Love draws all that we have within us to the action in which we are involved. It brings trust and acceptance; it heightens the senses; it allows us to be completely immersed in our work," M. P. Chase writes in *Just Being at the Piano*. "Love does not bring forth censorship and defensiveness, conditions that adversely affect our learning ability. It allows self-acceptance and total involvement." Playing the flute brings joy and light and beauty to my daily life.

Being an amateur gives me freedom to do what I wish with my musical talent. I can make mistakes, play less than perfectly, and allow myself to grow by the very process of learning to accept my imperfections. (I learned early in my life to be highly self-critical and to berate myself for the slightest error.)

Artists must constantly guard against these hidden expectations that flap around their natural gift like dark birds. They must focus instead on polishing the jewels already in hand. In this lies salvation from a fearful life, and for musicians, the way to actual music. Enter the polishing! Love the refining of mere vibration, those waves on your very shore. You can latch onto a single musical sound as if it were a material ray flying you through frightened air. The ray will guide you. It is the "it" we all have, and it is enough.

—W. A. Mathieu, *The Listening Book*

It's taken a long time, but now I can blow off a mistake casually. I believe in my heart of hearts that the spirit I put into my music is received by the listener; even with an occasional wrong note, my music is a gift to my soul and to the world. "Your own music is the child of your heart and you are entitled to love it, not because it's good but because it's part of you," Stephanie Judy writes in *Making Music for the Joy of It*. "All amateur musicians embrace a common task: We are not here to play music perfectly but to love music deeply."

I feel free, as an amateur, to let my creativity guide me to unusual ways of doing things. I'm not bound by the restrictions of formality or proper etiquette. I can be as silly or unconventional as I wish.

The amount of talent I have is not as important as my desire to create lovely sound. I believe that because I've been given a yearning to make music, I've also been given the ability to do so. As Mathieu writes in *The Musical Life*, "How can I wake up to what I have? becomes the question, not How much do I have? You have what you need."

Catherine Drinker Bowen puts it this way in *Friends and Fiddlers*:

I know what these people want; I have seen them pick up my violin and turn it over in their hands. They may not know it themselves, but they want music not by the ticket-ful, the purse-ful, but music as it should be had, music at home, a part of daily life, a thing as necessary, as satisfying, as the midday meal. They want to play. And they are kept back by the absurd, the mistaken, the wicked notion that in order to play an instrument one must be possessed by that bogey called Talent.

As an amateur musician, I feel special, aware that I can do something many people wish they could do. I get hugs, respect, gratitude, attention, praise, support, recognition, joy. Do I get million-dollar recording contracts? Is my name in lights at a major concert hall? Am I interviewed for public television? No. But I've matured enough to know that love and personal connections nurture my soul more deeply and sweetly than fame or fortune ever could.

I certainly don't love myself much when I'm impatient with a store clerk or too lazy to do the laundry, but I love myself when I play the flute. I respect myself for having the discipline to practice. I admire my willingness to be vulnerable in front of an audience. I appreciate my inner strength that allows me to take constructive criticism from my teacher.

Because I'm an amateur, I don't have to struggle with my ego. I can let go of competitiveness. I can take a guilt-free break from practicing when I'm on vacation. I can engage in other activities in my life that interest me.

Sure, I occasionally wonder what would have happened if I'd had a better flute teacher when I was young, and I regret not having practiced more. Sometimes I think, "Gee, I wish I could play as well as. . . ." But most of the time, I'm eternally grateful to the guiding angels who have led me to be who I am today. I feel exactly right being an amateur flutist. Music is sweet joy and sustenance to me, not the source of payment for my groceries and rent.

> I dare to think it is a gracious gift that enables the musician . . . to believe in a magic that can bring order and beauty into the world. Deluded your amateur musician may be, but happy he certainly is, because for him the road always goes on, for him, still ahead but in plain sight, there are water and green trees and the mountains of all delight.
> —Gerald W. Johnson, *A Little Night Music*

Music for the Love of It, August 1995

Street Musicians

When my husband, Fred, and I travel, we often stop and listen to street musicians. During the last year I have sought them out, pen and pad in hand, saying I was a writer for a national newsletter for amateur musicians. Some of them seemed to think I was famous.

Spring found me in Seattle, listening to a small man playing the pennywhistle on a busy street across from the Pike Place Market. He wore brown slacks, a yellow T-shirt, and a straw hat. His beaded necklace had a saxophone charm as its centerpiece. Danny Khobo is from Capetown, South Africa. Since 1985, he has been playing flute and saxophone with the International Children's Festival, which brought him to Seattle. When he's not working with the festival, he earns extra money with his pennywhistle, making music for passersby, as he does most of the year all over South Africa. He plays African music called Kwela, a little jazz, and original tunes.

He told me with great enthusiasm that his music and the people who listen to it keep him healthy. Although he is 49 years old, he looks about 30, and he says this is because of the encouragement people give him and because he does what's most important—playing music. He said, "Music is healing, like medicine. It's a spiritual thing like meditation. I close my eyes, and the sound just comes to my fingertips. It's very calming."

Danny was 8 years old when he started on pennywhistle. Later he worked in the diamond mines, where a friend, in two weeks' time, taught him the C-major scale on the sax. From there, Danny taught himself. As for his earnings, he said, "I have everything I need. If I want something but I don't have enough to buy it, I wait. Then I always get it."

My favorite cousins live in South Africa, and I wondered if they had ever passed Danny on the streets of their native Johannesburg. After he performed a Kwela piece especially for me, I dropped some money into his box, and as I walked away, he called to me, "I'm so happy. I'll never forget you."

On another day in Seattle, at a busy downtown intersection near a mall, I heard a bagpipe and drums. I followed the sound until I saw two clean-cut college-age boys in kilts on a corner. When I asked them why they were doing this, their answer was brief: "Kicks and cash." They told me that they hate each other (which was obviously not true) and that they make an "obscene amount of money" (which I was inclined to believe). Nathan, the bagpiper, a university student from Victoria, British Columbia, said they attract a lot of attention because of the bagpipe; its popularity is growing, and new music is being written for it. The other musician, Grant, plays snare drum in the City of Victoria Band. They said they busk together during school breaks, then explained that "busking" is a Canadian and British term that means playing on the street. When I asked about their experiences busking, Nathan answered, "People ask me what's under my kilt. I don't answer. Then they lift it up and find out for themselves." Grant's answer was that in Ottawa last summer a girl got up after a song, kissed him on the lips, and ran away. As I walked away smiling, a group of school children yelled at Grant and Nathan, "Don't stop! Play more! More!"

On my next visit to the Pike Place Market, I found a couple performing popular songs, the male playing a guitar, the female doing vocals, harmonizing beautifully. During a break, Mark told me he had always played the guitar in his off-hours. At work, he couldn't wait to get home to his guitar. Finally, he felt he could no longer "waste time" at work, so he quit his job, and now he and his friend busk five hours every day. Some days they make good money, while other days they earn $5 all day. "We have enough money to get by, and it's better than working at McDonald's."

In Washington, D.C., I came across a group of eight middle-aged men singing their hearts out about a block from the Smithsonian, accompanied by a single guitar and the sounds of the nearby water fountain and traffic. A huge political protest was taking place that day on the Mall. The guitar player, his grey hair in a long ponytail, told me that the group is from North Carolina (about two hours from where I live), and that they travel to where there are big gatherings, so they may witness for God. "We're not professionals and aren't trying to be. Our music is simply an inoffensive way to share the gospel. Music passes your mind and goes to your heart. We don't accept money. We get a lot of fulfillment, meeting people on a heart-to-heart basis."

I wandered onto the Mall, where hundreds of thousands of people were milling about in preparation for the march. The atmosphere was electric and energetic. I spotted three boys playing rap music, using torn Rubbermaid plastic garbage cans as drums. The rap went on . . . and on . . . and on. Finally, they came up for air. James, Keeven, and Jeran are 14, 16, and 16, respectively. They play on weekends and during summers and are saving the money they earn to buy real drums and equipment so they can turn professional. They call themselves the "Young Nations." None of the three boys has a mother living at home, but they say that their fathers are proud of them for their music. They were eager to get back to their music, and as I contributed a little to their future purchases, the pulse of their rap started up again.

In Edinburgh, Scotland, I met The Earthlings, who claimed they came from outer space. They are four young men in their mid-20s—two on guitar, one on double bass, and one on drums, along with high-tech mikes and an amp—who have known each other for a very long time. I asked what their most interesting experience has been while busking. One of them answered, "We're on a mission from God (with snickering by the other members). Once we witnessed a miracle. It was an overcast day. A guy in a wheelchair came over to us. A ray of sunshine appeared and shone on us all. Then he got up from his wheelchair, walked a few steps, and put a lot of money in our box." I asked how much they made. "We can make £160 (about $250) in three to four hours, and we usually drink it that night." They characterize their music as "rock-a-belly Presley, hillbilly street music." When I asked about the tattoos three of them sported, they said they draw them on every day. They looked at the fourth guy, who wasn't saying much, and added, "His is in a private place."

The next group I spoke to comprised four guys from different countries who had just met recently in a work camp for the International Volunteer Service—Universal Folk Song Society. They were college students from Germany, Italy, Belgium, and England who had been playing Ceilidh music, traditional Scottish folk dances, in concert. Their instruments were a tambourine, a harmonica, a guitar, a fiddle, and their voices. Their two favorite parts of busking were watching women dance to their music and watching people throw coins in their box. All of them busk regularly at home for extra income.

In the autumn, Freddy and I went to our favorite place in the world, Santa Fe, New Mexico. I don't often see street musicians there, but this time a middle-aged man was playing guitar and singing in the outdoor Plaza downtown. Juan Bermudez, part Mexican, part Navajo, was darkskinned, wore his hair in a ponytail, and had on a tie-dyed shirt and boots. He sings for about two hours each day because he enjoys it. In Santa Fe, he told me, people are arrested for playing on the street for money. He got started in music when he won a talent show in the first grade. To make his living he gives massages, makes jewelry, and does stonework. He used to make music for money but didn't like to be in bars. He plays mostly his own music, ballads that relate to conditions in the world or to his personal life. When he is in love, he expresses his love, concern, and frustration more intimately through his music than through words. Once his kneecaps were shattered, and he ended up in a body cast for five months. "Music was my therapy," he said. The music he writes "doesn't belong to me—it's channeled through me."

When I was in London in the winter, I sought out a music store to browse through, looking for flute music, as always. This time, a now-familiar term caught my eye: busking. I was amazed to find: *101 Folk Songs for Buskers*, *101 Showtunes for Buskers*, *101 Australian Songs for Buskers*, *101 Pub Favorites*, *101 Country Hits for Buskers*, *Busking for Special Occasions*, *Busker Club*, and many more.

It was in London, too, that I saw my favorite busker, at the bottom of a long, steep escalator in the Underground, London's subway. He was dressed in a hilarious cat costume, playing high-energy jazz on a trumpet, dancing to the beat, and accompanied by a full backup band on tape. It was a perfect location, giving people the opportunity to get out money while they rode down the crowded escalator. I wanted to stop and talk to the musician, but I was too busy with my cousins from South Africa. Talking and laughing, listening to wonderful music, we ascended the escalator to the street.

Music for the Love of It, April 1994

Happiness is More Important:
The Story of Katherine Kemler

ate again! I pulled up to the airport terminal, tires screeching, and rushed inside. I'd only met Katherine Kemler once, briefly, but I immediately recognized the well-dressed, self-assured woman, luggage at her feet, calmly reading a book.

"Hello, Katherine," I said. She looked up at me with a big smile. "Hi. My friends call me Penny."

We did the typical chatter—"How was your flight? What's the weather like at home?"—as we loaded her bags into my car, but by the time we'd negotiated the ramps leading to the exit and were cruising down Interstate 40, we were into intimate talk about men, husbands, and our respective marriages—a warmth and trust that was to become the hallmark of our friendship.

Penny stayed in our home that weekend in 2000, giving a flute seminar and mini-recital for my students. We went to my aerobics class together, enjoyed my husband's home-cooked meals, and tried out each other's flutes. I liked Penny's vivacious, engaging, upbeat personality immensely and was so entertained by her adventurous life that when she returned last week to be the guest artist for our local flute fair, I asked if I could write an article about her.

She responded, "What would be so interesting about my life?" Astounded after having heard one exciting tale after another, I set out to encapsulate her life thus far. Penny, are you listening?

Penny grew up in a suburb of Washington, D.C., with parents who were not especially musical. She decided to play an instrument in the fourth grade because the music students got out of class for 30 minutes each week and won medals in music competitions. The flute, made of silver and held transversely, attracted her by its difference.

When she entered her first solo and ensemble festival after about a year of study, she lost her place in the music three times and was so nervous she wet her pants. But she won the first of the wished-for medals.

She began flute lessons with Mark Thomas at age 13 and decided at 16 to major in music. Oberlin College accepted Penny on the basis of her grades and SAT scores, but she had not applied as a flute student. She simply showed up one day at flute professor Robert Willoughby's office, not realizing the competitive nature of the music conservatory's admission policies. Mr. Willoughby listened to her play and accepted her as a student nevertheless.

Penny continued graduate studies with flute professor Sam Baron at the State University of New York at Stony Brook. As she told Ervin Monroe for his article in *The American Piper*, "Sam Baron was a great teacher and human being. He helped me to believe in myself and made me feel that I had something to offer the music world."* One of the highlights in her life was her trip to the New College Summer Music Festival in Sarasota, Florida, where she performed as second flute soloist with Mr. Baron and the great violinist Joseph Silverstein.

After receiving her Master of Music degree, she freelanced and then was accepted to Tanglewood for the summer of 1976, where she played under legendary conductors Leonard Bernstein, Seiji Ozawa, and Colin Davis. While there, she was offered a teaching position at the University of Wyoming. "I wasn't even sure where Wyoming was and had to look it up in the encyclopedia," she said. "As we were landing in Laramie, I looked out the window and saw . . . nothing. I vowed to stay only three years, but ended up living there for 11." She enjoyed teaching some good students and had frequent and varied performing opportunities. "Some of the towns were quite small, but every chance to perform is a valuable experience, and I was able to experiment with new repertoire."

After her first year, Penny was promoted to assistant professor and assigned to teach Music Appreciation to a class of 300 students. She says the entire football team, ski team, and various cowboys sat in the back, chewing tobacco and spitting it on the floor. But Penny made it her mission to make the class interesting, inviting guest speakers, the university orchestra, and an opera company to make presentations. Some students later told her they had actually enjoyed the classical music, but that they'd never admit it to anyone else!

Penny married a zoology professor in 1982 in what she calls a real Western-style wedding, with a stagecoach ride from the church to the reception. They spent their first year in Oxford, England, for her hus-

*Ervin Monroe, "From Cowpoke to Cajun: Katherine Kemler Tells Her Story," *The American Piper*, 1999/2000. Quoted with permission of the author.

band's post-doc, so Penny seized the opportunity to work towards her doctorate, studying with William Bennett and Adrian Brett.

Their son Jonathan was born in 1985. After her marriage ended in 1987, Penny and Jonathan moved to Baton Rouge, Louisiana, having been offered the flute professorship at Louisiana State University that same year. Penny still works at LSU and says, "Every teaching day is a joy."

In 1995, Penny received an invitation to teach for two weeks and perform in Beijing, China. She found the Central Conservatory of Music "like some kind of war zone. Dirty, with no air conditioning. Many windows were broken, and there were some very interesting smells." The flute professors spoke no English, and the official translator didn't show up, so a student tried to translate Penny's masterclass. "I kept telling jokes, and everyone sat stone-faced. I thought, either these people have no sense of humor or I'm not being translated properly!" Subsequent masterclasses went better when a new translator was found.

Penny had thought that her recital would take place at the conservatory, but she then learned that the venue would be the huge Beijing Concert Hall. News of the concert was trumpeted in all the papers. Penny had planned a program of mostly avant-garde pieces to interest the students. Here's how she tells the story:

"I don't think the Chinese audience liked any of the contemporary pieces I played, but I ended with the Genin *Carnival of Venice*, and they loved that. They wanted an encore, but I had not prepared one, so I played the last variation of the Genin again. They wanted another encore and would not stop clapping. Finally, I went out and played *Syrinx* from memory. I don't think they liked that either, but at least they stopped clapping and I could leave."

Despite the unexpected adventures, Penny had a wonderful time and was delighted to return to China in 1997 at the invitation of the Shanghai Conservatory. She began to study Mandarin and this time could communicate her basic needs to her hosts. Penny rehearsed with her accompanist without a translator because she had learned the words for *faster*, *slower*, *louder*, *softer*, and so on, and she taught masterclasses for many hours each day to highly advanced students. She was also pleased to hear a variety of repertoire in this part of the country and perceive an open attitude toward 20th-century music.

During that same trip, Penny visited Hong Kong, where she was interviewed on Hong Kong Radio and gave a masterclass and recital at the Hong Kong Academy for the Performing Arts. This beautiful school had wonderful facilities but mostly technically weak flute students. An assigned accompanist from a local music store could not play Penny's music. After receiving help to "phone every decent pianist in Hong Kong," she located a pianist who was able to learn the difficult Franck *Sonata in A Major* in only two days. The sold-out concert went beautifully.

During this trip, Penny woke up one morning to find a huge canker sore on the underside of her tongue. Although she continued her activities as usual, when it didn't go away, she consulted her dentist and seven doctors over the course of seven months, and most told her it was nothing to worry about. Finally, she had a biopsy. Carcinoma in situ. Part of her tongue would have to be removed. The diagnosis was particularly dismaying for a flutist, of course, and surprising because Penny had lived in a healthful way, eaten well, exercised, and never smoked or chewed tobacco. The surgery showed squamous cell cancer, which spreads quickly and can be fatal. Terrified, Penny sought opinions and had further surgery only two weeks after the first operation. This time the doctors got clear results. During the following year, Penny experienced more scares, another biopsy, and enlarged lymph nodes. However, subsequent tests have been clear, and Penny has regained all her ability on the flute.

Although that time in her life was a nightmare, Penny says that many blessings came to her. She re-examined her life and her priorities.

"It changed life from the inside. I felt different. It's not every day that you look at your own mortality, and that's scary. I started to take things less for granted and appreciate things more. I'd often not even notice the flowers and the trees, little things like that. Now I take a minute to notice the tulips in bloom. It has made me grateful for everything I have—to be able to play the flute at all, because I was facing the possibility that my surgery would affect my playing negatively or prevent me from playing.

"The experience made me realize how important family is. Before, I was goal-oriented and wanted to get further in my career. I've become less competitive. I'd hear someone younger than I play great, and I'd feel bad about my limitations. But now I've accepted my own imperfections more, and when I hear others who are better, instead of feeling threatened, I feel inspired and joyous in their success."

Penny genuinely likes people and enjoys hearing their stories. "Everything's better if you can share it with another person," she says. "I believe in being open with people, because nothing's accomplished by hiding things. I believe in sharing. I've heard of teachers who want to keep their teaching or performing tricks a secret. If I learn something, I want to tell my students immediately and be as helpful as I can.

"Confrontation is difficult," she says. "If I'm angry with someone, it's hard to bring that up. Even with students, I'm really good at 'Great job,

I'm so proud of you,' but I dislike saying, 'You know this is the third week and you haven't practiced.' I agonize over those conversations and seek to get my message across without losing control or being harmful.

"Sometimes I talk with students about failures in my career. One season, I played in a professional ensemble. I auditioned the following year, expecting to return because the audition committee had clearly shown they loved me, but I didn't get rehired. Did I play a poor audition? I was told that the conductor didn't like me so they couldn't hire me again no matter how I played. If I tell my students that story, they're helped to face disappointments in their own lives—they can see that this is what life is like."

Penny fell in love with composer Paul Hayden in 1987 in Baton Rouge, but he left to take an associate professorship at Eastern Illinois University. For 10 years, they maintained a long-distance relationship. Neither wanted to give up the tenure and salary that each had worked so hard to achieve. After the cancer, Penny realized that life is short and read about the idea that we should all live as though we had only one year left. She asked herself, "What's wrong with this picture—that we're so far away from each other?" She made a decision almost overnight to ask him to marry her and come back to live in Baton Rouge.

Right before Christmas 1997 she popped the big question, "feeling good in my heart, knowing what I'd done was right, even if he said no." On Christmas Day, Paul said yes, and they've just celebrated their fifth anniversary. "I kicked myself for taking so long to make myself so happy," says Penny, "but this is one way that the cancer was a blessing in disguise."

"I was on the judging panel last summer for the NFA Young Artist Competition. The judges had some disagreement, so we spoke individually about what we liked and didn't like about each finalist. I realized, 'It doesn't matter what you do, somebody is not going to like it.' I found that freeing! I might as well play to please myself and have a good time."

Penny, a deeply spiritual person, recognizes how fragile life is and tries to enjoy every minute of every day. She says that she's more grateful for everything now and that performing has become more joyful. "I try to play music for God's glory and not my own. Reaching age 50 was magical because suddenly it became more important to be a good person than to be a great flutist, more important to be happy than be famous. It's easier now to let go. It may not be the way I wanted, but everything always comes out for the best."

Katherine Kemler has released three CDs on the Centaur label, and she has commissioned and premiered *Soliloquy* by Lowell Liebermann as well as two pieces by husband Paul Hayden, *A Tre* and *Grand Mamou*. Last year, Penny was honored to become the Carl Prince Matthies Professor of Flute, an endowed professorship at LSU. She continues to perform, teach, and radiate her love of life wherever she goes.

Penny, are you listening? You're a special gift to the flute world and to all who know you.

The Flutist Quarterly, Summer 2003

From the Heart

Music helps us recognize something un-nameable within us. An energy flows between the music maker and the listener—between friends and strangers, even between people who have lost their most basic connections to the world and to others. The music itself is the bridge, and when the music ignites the energy within us, it can be a joyful and profound experience. These stories describe times when I experienced that recognition and was touched by that intimate yet universal connection.

Intimacy in Music Making

When I perform, the gift I offer comprises not only the notes, melodies, and sound, but also my inner being, my heart and soul, the essence of me. Turning loose this precious internal treasure into the world beyond my skin feels risky. What if those I play for don't appreciate my music? If they see my pain, will they think I'm weak? If my joy shows, will they be jealous? If I make a mistake, will they laugh? *What if they just don't like me?*

Intimacy is the freedom to be totally ourselves in the presence of another. Intimacy means letting another person see our darkest, most wounded selves, as well as our unreserved blazing beauty and grace. In an intimate moment, we're vulnerable because we remove the mask that we wear to function and survive in the world.

Intimacy can be created through meaningful eye contact, touch, sex, sharing a profound experience, or the making of music. True intimacy is not easily expressed in words, and one of the lovely aspects of music is that it goes beyond words. "Music is sound coded for human purposes—a secret password that opens the borders between us," as author W. A. Mathieu writes in *The Listening Book*.

We need intimacy to be emotionally and spiritually healthy, but intimate feelings can be so intense and sometimes uncomfortable that we often fear them. If I push through my fear and allow myself to open, I always find a reward. The "high" I often feel after a performance comes from a sense of immediate closeness and eternal oneness. An intangible yet real connection is made, the feeling of separation ceases, and I feel a part of all life. "Inside your personal reality is universal reality," Mathieu writes. "If we penetrate the utterly personal we connect with everyone."

Effective musical communication results in and requires intimacy. Brooks de Wetter-Smith, an international concert artist, says that he consciously creates intimacy during performances by playing to his accompanist or to someone in the audience. He believes that "the emotional connection between people is what makes artists, musicians, and writers what they are. Without that emotional intensity in the player *and his connection to someone else*, the performance is empty."

Other soloists find intimacy through different channels. Larry Krantz, a Canadian freelance flutist and teacher explains, "I've never felt intimacy with the audience as much as with the composer. In attempting to perceive the music with the same understanding as the composer comes a feeling of looking into his or her soul. If there is intimacy it's more where the audience has been invited to share in a conversation between the composer and me."

One of my students, a psychiatrist, last year found herself in the unusual position of playing in a student recital with one of her former patients in the audience. "We were forced to step out of our roles. Our sense of each other became enlarged. His hearing me play allowed him to know more about me than if we had run into each other on the street and chatted."

Music lessons are another arena in which intimacy plays an important role. I often sound my worst during lessons, because my teacher asks me to stretch my musical limits, and I have to struggle to try to accomplish what he asks. I must be willing to let my teacher see my incompetence, impatience, and embarrassment.

In addition, my lessons take place in a small studio behind a closed door. My teacher is a man, and I'm a woman, and there we are, scrutinizing each other's lips to learn about embouchure, touching each other's fingers to improve hand position, placing our hands on each other's abdomens to feel proper breathing mechanics. These are behaviors that I would not ordinarily engage in with any man other than my husband, yet if I want to learn from this particular instructor, I have to dive into this intimate place with him and swim.

Larry Krantz agrees: "Nothing can be more intimate or intimidating than taking a lesson. When I play for a teacher for the first time it's very much like walking into a room with a stranger, stripping away all of the veneer and exposing every part of my being—the good and the bad. Good teachers are experienced with this fact and work to set the naked student at ease as quickly as possible, to be able to accomplish something in the lesson. As time passes and the comfort zone increases, a deeper trust and understanding begins to develop in both teacher and student, and so does the effectiveness of the teaching. It is essential for the student and teacher to get emotionally close for the student to learn and the teacher to deliver ideas to the student."

Our true inner selves, so often hidden from view, are eager to be seen, known, and loved. Making music is one way to satisfy that deep human need if we're willing to go beyond our fear. I want to stay deeply connected to people for the rest of my life, and I hope to play my flute until my last breath.

Music for the Love of It, October 1996

A Magical Musical Partnership

An air of excitement pervades the concert hall. The lights look too bright from the stage, the microphones seem too close, and a flock of butterflies is playing a lively game of racquetball in my stomach. Julie, at the piano, waits for me to begin. I raise my flute to my lips. I look into Julie's eyes. The most important part of the concert happens in this moment, before the music starts.

When I look into Julie's eyes, I feel my soul. In the flash of an instant, I remember Who really plays the music, and for Whom I really perform. I have a sense, beyond words or thoughts, that the God of my understanding is watching over us. I feel safe and calm; I become joy.

When Julie's eyes and mine lock in that moment, we connect on a level far deeper than either of us can understand or explain. Our souls twirl around each other and lose their boundaries so that the music seems to come from one instrument, not two. Both of us are reminded that we are not doing this scary, intimate, vulnerable act alone; we have each other. The Source of the music wants us to do this, it is so right, and we are blessed, along with those who listen.

I have played with other pianists and with guitarists, violinists, and organists. Because I love it, playing my flute is almost always fun and interesting and beautiful. But the magic I feel with Julie is unique in my experience, so I know that she and I share something very special. We have come to believe that we are "musical soul-mates," that each is a profound teacher and partner to the other.

Julie has been the primary catalyst for helping me to become a solo performer. Her enthusiasm and willingness to spend time rehearsing, and her appreciation of the beauty of my playing, have nurtured my self-confidence, creativity, and initiative. She is a talented composer who has written and arranged many pieces for flute and piano, gifts from her heart to mine. The opportunity to perform has sparked my desire to improve, which is why I am now taking lessons again. I am practicing a great deal and making progress because of Julie's encouragement.

Similarly, I have been the inspiration for Julie to blossom as a composer and musician. Before she and I met, she had not composed music for 10 years. Her first love, music, had been put aside so that she could raise her children and develop a professional career in computer science. Although my ability to compose is nonexistent, I have good ideas, so I might say to Julie, "Wouldn't it be great to do a special flute and piano version of such-and-such a song?" Often it's not long before Julie produces a gorgeous arrangement. During the past year, she has also written some exquisite original pieces for flute and piano, because she now has a vehicle for showcasing her music. Occasionally, while she's in the process of composing, she tells me that she's out of ideas or that nothing is working. My response to her is usually something like, "What do you mean, you have no ideas? What about that beautiful theme you played for me last week? Get back to that theme! It's fabulous!" Sometimes she needs a little "kick in the butt." Sometimes I need a little kick from her to get up on stage and perform. We do that for each other; musical soulmates help each other grow. The response to our music from audiences, newspaper critics, and our friends has been tremendous.

People notice the chemistry between Julie and me. They approach us after we play a recital or at church, remarking about the spark between us at least as often as they comment about the music itself. Such remarks have become such a consistent pattern that we are convinced that the chemistry is very real, not just the result of one particular performance. The experience feels very internal, so I'm always surprised that people perceive the love and oneness between us.

Trust plays a large role in this relationship. I trust Julie to take the music at the right tempo, to find me if I get lost, to remember to give me time to breathe between notes if I need it. Julie trusts me to advise her about the capabilities of the flute and to tell her truthfully whether or not her compositions are good. She trusts me to not take the spotlight for myself, to acknowledge her as a true musical partner, not merely as an accompanist.

The magic pervades our rehearsals as well. When we need to go back to a particular passage, frequently we both know exactly which measure the other wants to start with, almost like ESP. Often, we independently choose the same pieces to include on a particular concert program. Once we came up with very different ideas for a program. The hardest challenge we've faced in the three years of this relationship was to resolve that difference. After quite a bit of tense discussion, I deferred to her opinion, and the concert was perfect.

We spend a significant amount of time at these supposed musical rehearsals just talking, sharing our lives, laughing and sometimes crying. We have become friends who enrich each other's life in many ways. During the weeks when we're too busy to meet, we miss making music and feel a deep longing to play with each other, almost like lovers who long to be together after a separation. We are meant to create music together during this time in our lives. Maybe the magic won't last forever. But for now, I soak up every minute of joy, every note of music, every spark of love and spirit, with deep gratitude and awareness of the gift of being alive.

Music for the Love of It, August 1992

Bars Behind Bars

*L*ast fall I gave the worst concert of my life, in a hall without air conditioning on a blazingly hot day. Ceiling fans and towering floor fans created a necessary movement of the stifling air but distorted the sound of my flute and blew my sheet music to the floor. I had to strain to hear the pianist, who played on an upright that was missing a C-sharp. Every few minutes, an announcement blasted from loudspeakers. Background noise came from an institutional kitchen preparing dinner, a cacophony that reached a crescendo as a huge pot crashed to the floor. Control of dynamics was not an option—I couldn't hear my own tone, and I hit more wrong notes than I have in decades. Out of those conditions arose a radiance so powerful that now, months later, I remember that performance in a prison dining hall as the grandest of my life.

The concert was the outcome of a letter I wrote almost a year ago, acting on a strong urge to communicate with a member of my church who is incarcerated. (I'll call him Anthony.) When he responded, we began an ongoing correspondence that has explored and deepened the connection between us. Anthony grew up in abject poverty as the youngest of 11 children and was virtually illiterate when he committed a crime at age 18.

During his 24-year incarceration, Anthony discovered a driving force within that compelled him to turn his life around. He began by obtaining his GED, then graduated from college *magna cum laude*. He awakened spiritually and became a sincere seeker of the divine. He is now preparing for graduate school and dreams of becoming the director of a nonprofit organization dedicated to the prevention of crime among juveniles and youths. Anthony transformed himself from a broken child to an eloquent, dignified man whose eyes shine with intelligence and goodness that come from the depths of the soul.

As I came to know Anthony, I began to visit him in prison. From those visits rose my desire to bring live music to him and his fellow inmates. My friends and musical partners, Julie Harris and Leslie Carol, were eager to join me. So was our minister, the Reverend Nancy Oristaglio, and friend Greg McCallum, who came along for the concert. My motives for reaching out to the prisoners rose from my belief that the essential nature of every human being is good. People aren't born bad, but they do bad things. Sometimes they've been so hurt, abused, neglected, or poorly taught that their truth and beauty are buried under terrible ugliness.

Our concert hall (a prison dining room) was filled with people who, in some cases, have done unspeakably horrible things, but my friends and I were there to play music, not to make judgments about the audience. My personal choice is to keep an open mind and look for the goodness inside everyone. I'm not condoning crimes, nor do I think criminals should be turned loose, but I want to see even lawbreakers as multi-dimensional.

Before the concert began, Anthony introduced me. Then, between our pieces—which were mostly pop, Broadway, and jazz—I spoke to the men, asked them questions, and invited them to question me. At first, few responded to my invitation, but perhaps they noticed that I wasn't preaching or talking about morals. I trusted that God's universal, transcendent music would deliver a message to each man's heart. The men began to introduce themselves, and soon we were chatting and laughing like casual friends.

One of them asked how long I'd been studying my instrument. Another wondered what a beginning flutist sounded like, and I mimicked a child playing "Twinkle, Twinkle," slowly and haltingly. That elicited some chuckling. Someone commented on how I made it look easy and asked how long Julie, Leslie, and I have played together. (Twelve years.) Another asked if I'd produced any CDs. I looked right at him and said, "No, but I will if you'll be my agent, producer, and backer." The room exploded in laughter. The positive energy and oneness continued to grow until I thought my heart would burst with joy.

A young man sat with Rev. Nancy, and they held a Bible between them, engrossed in quiet but intense conversation. Later, as they held hands tightly, the man bowed his head, and Nancy reassured him that he was a whole, perfect, beloved child of God. When they finished the prayer, they hugged, and I was dazzled by the man's face, illuminated with joy, comfort, and peace. Tears came to my own eyes as I felt my love for my minister, admired her powerful ability to bestow such depth of healing, and experienced gratitude that she and I and our friends had done something so wonderful this day.

The music brought us together and uplifted us. Even though most of the life circumstances of the inmates are vastly unlike mine, music cut through our differences and became a common language. An ignored verbal message can be communicated intensely and powerfully through the medium of music. Greg played a spur-of-the-moment ragtime piano solo that riveted the audience, reminding me that deep emotions can be shared by folks who are highly divergent socioeconomically or educationally.

We'd brought food for the men, donated by generous friends, and I invited the inmates to help themselves. At first I thought there was way too much; however, the entire table was completely cleared of every cookie crumb and drop of soda within ten minutes. Sixty men attended the concert, which Anthony told me was much higher attendance than is usual for the programs in this unit.

The inmates couldn't do enough for us. When I spilled my water, someone cheerfully wiped the floor and brought me another glass. Another inmate carried my bags, and another brought me the empty platters. Everyone asked us to return. I wanted to go back immediately. I don't know if my heart has ever been so big with love or so moved. I don't know whether the joy pulsing through my body has ever been as alive. When have I felt so blessed, so overcome with humility, gratitude, and awe?

Anthony wrote me a letter afterwards, saying, "Your concert was well attended and received by the inmates because it allowed a new medium through which love and inspiration were conveyed. The music and your and your friends' presence was clearly a demonstration of love, rather than an instillation of fear. Your golden flute and Julie's piano playing created an unmistakable vibration of love and unity emanating directly from your souls. Through the music, the inmates got a deep and distinct feeling that they were being embraced by a spiritual being."

I don't believe this could've been achieved through any other medium. In music, no judgment exists. In music, no one is good or bad, better or worse, higher or lower. We simply are.

The most meaningful moment of the afternoon—one I'll remember forever—happened near the end of our performance while I was counting several measures of rests as Julie played the piano. I scanned the attentive faces in the audience, wanting to hold in my lap the little child in each of them. When my gaze fell on Anthony, our eyes locked. He silently mouthed, "I love you." My lips formed the words, "Me, too."

As the bars of music soared into hearts and minds, the steel bars dissolved. The distance between "them" and "us" was no more. Anthony wrote, "I allowed the music to penetrate my being, and myself to be inundated by its melody so that at points during the concert I fantasized that the moment would last for eternity."

Spirit Express, Newsletter of the Unity Center
of Peace, October 2001

My 50th Birthday Concert

My 50th birthday concert surpassed my highest expectations. I opened with *Ode to Joy*, taking advantage of the big pipe organ in the church because, as I told everyone, I wanted to start with the happiest piece I could think of.

A few months ago my younger brother had asked me, "Aren't you depressed about turning 50?" I answered, "NO! I'm so happy and grateful to have been given so many days and years of life to experience love, joy, sorrow, loss, the whole array of human experience."

As I prepared for my concert, several people commented that they admired or were surprised by how openly I publicized my age. Our culture teaches us that it's bad to grow older, that it's not cool to be old, and that it's best to keep our age a secret. I feel that every day that we're alive on this earth is a gift from God, so I haven't subscribed to that philosophy. I'm grateful that God has given me 50 years in which to grow, learn, suffer, love, appreciate, and be joyful.

Many people don't ever live to be 50. The majority of my extended family, including little children, were killed by the Nazis. God has granted me health, strength, and half a century to slowly allow divine light to shine more brightly within me, and to deepen my ability to love and be loved. How can I despair about getting older? Every day provides another opportunity to choose a higher way of living.

When Rev. Nancy blesses the children in our church every Sunday and affirms that they're safe and protected, little tears prick behind my eyes. I grew up terrified of loss, abandonment, and lack of safety, because of the stories my parents told of their time in hiding and in concentration camps. Every Sunday, Rev. Nancy reminds me that I'm safe and protected, too: that God is watching over me and that all is well. That's why I'm not afraid or embarrassed to say that I've reached the ripe old age of 50. I'm proud of it, and happy, and boundlessly grateful.

I was honored to play with my friends Greg McCallum, a concert pianist, and Julie Harris, a pianist and composer. It was a joy to make music with them. Greg played *Happy Birthday Variations* on the piano (a Ya-maha seven-foot grand that he'd brought to the hall for this event!). He also played *Now Thank We All Our God* on the organ while Mark Malachi performed the most beautiful, awesome interpretive dance of gratitude you can imagine. Leslie Rinehart joined Julie and me for a love song to my husband, Fred.

I absolutely loved playing on my brand new gold flute. I feel awed to have such a beautiful instrument, and guess what the serial number is? 50!

During the concert, I shared my musical journey—how I've struggled and grown and how happy I am to have a life in music. Throughout the evening, I noticed people crying. My encore, *The Gartan Mother's Lullaby*, was almost everyone's favorite piece of the evening. I asked everyone to imagine a mother's love for her child, to feel that love in their own heart, and to pass that love to everyone in the room and to all the world.

"If we all could do that every day," I said, "that would be the best birthday gift of all." During that piece, I don't think there was a dry eye in the house. My notes, tone and intonation weren't perfect—not even close—but I guess the Spirit of the music got through to them.

We had a reception afterward, and I was given tons and tons of gifts and flowers. Earlier in the day, Freddy and I and my friends who had come from England, Syracuse, and Vancouver, stopped at the florist to pick up the flower arrangement Freddy had ordered for me. I got out of the car, and so did everyone else. I thought to myself, "Now, why in the world do they think it takes four grown men and a woman to carry one flower arrangement to the car?"

Inside, the florist handed me *two* arrangements. I read the card attached to the second arrangement, which was signed by James Galway.

My mouth dropped open about a foot, my eyes popped out about eight inches, and I was stunned into silence and wonder. Those beautiful flowers shone on the stage during the whole concert and will shine in my heart always.

One couple that I'd never met traveled six hours each way from northern Virginia to attend, and I was thrilled and honored that our friend "Anthony" (a prison inmate and church member who had received permission to attend) had come as well. This was the first Unity Church event he had ever attended.

One of the best gifts was from my 13-year-old student Adam Cutchin, who, now that he is growing into a man, won't hug "girls" like me. He was in the audience, and afterwards he came up to me with his arms raised for a big hug. That said more than speech ever could.

Thanks to everyone from Unity who helped—ushers, stagehands, the person who designed and printed the flyers and programs, and the folks who gave the reception.

Turning 50 by celebrating with music was mighty fine. My brother thinks I'm crazy, but then again, he's only 48.

Spirit Express, Newsletter of the Unity Center of Peace, October 2001

Feeding Myself with Music

People who look at me see a 5'6" woman whose weight is in normal proportion to her height. But most of the time, I feel fat. People tell me that I'm beautiful and attractive with my wavy brown hair, blue eyes, and clear complexion. It's only now, however, in my 40s, that I feel pretty, and then only some of the time. I have these distorted images of myself because I have an eating disorder. I'm a compulsive overeater, which means that rather than eating for energy or pleasure, I learned early in life to use large quantities of food (mostly sweets) to comfort myself when I was upset or to numb myself to avoid painful feelings. When I was younger, I was a "yo-yo" dieter, which resulted in frequent significant swings in weight. Thankfully, though, for over a decade I have been recovering from food addiction through various healing modalities. Most of the time, now, I eat moderately and healthfully, and I maintain a stable weight, because I continue to use, on a daily basis, the healing principles I've learned.

I have an easy time writing about my musical experiences in this public column because my life as a musician represents the part of me that is whole, creative, and healthy—the best of me. I feel scared and vulnerable writing about my eating disorder, which represents the shadow part of me that is sick, struggling, sorrowful, despairing, and in need of help. My courage and willingness to write on this private topic come from my belief that every human being has his or her own version of the shadow (although it may manifest itself differently) and from my commitment to express myself truthfully, in this column and in my life.

My eating disorder, if left unchecked, can interfere with my daily music practice in several ways. Because I play the flute, which requires diaphragmatic breathing, a day of overeating makes playing uncomfortable and significantly affects my breath control. At times, when overly stuffed with food, I've avoided practicing altogether, simply so that I wouldn't have to be acutely aware of the fullness of my body. When my physical and mental fitness is strong and alert, I can be creative with and through music, not by composing or improvising, but by playing pieces in un-usual arrangements, choosing perfect selections for different occasions, organizing ensembles and concerts, and finding ways to have fun with music. Too much food, especially too much sugar, drains my physical energy, dulls my mind, and blocks access to that wonderful creativity.

The pads underneath the keys in a flute can get sticky and cause the keys to make unwanted "tsk" sounds. Stickiness from the moisture of the breath is common, and that's why a flutist often uses a piece of ab-sorbent cigarette paper to remove the wetness. When a flutist has eaten sweets, the sugar in his or her breath gets into the pads; the hardened sugar can take weeks to clear out. I've sometimes practiced with the guilt of knowing that I was polluting my beloved flute, or with the awareness that the unwanted key sounds bothering me were caused by my own choice to engage in self-destructive and "flute-destructive" behavior.

At times, I've had to schedule my practice session several hours after meals, but because I eat more normally now, I can sometimes take up my flute soon after a meal. Conversely, I have difficulty playing when I'm very hungry, because I don't have enough physical energy or mental concentration. So before I begin my practice, I check in with my mind and body to assess whether I'm doing this at a time that feels right and good.

Every trial in life comes with a gift in its hand. Through the many years of trying to overcome my eating disorder, I've had to develop a high degree of intentional self-discipline and focus. Combating this ad-diction has created strengths in my character that have given me the im-petus to practice, improve, and grow. I use those strengths in practicing, improving, and growing in music, too, and the discipline I've learned through studying music has helped me on the road to recovery.

If I have to stay vigilant during ordinary days to balance healthy eat-ing and my practice of music, performance days require twice as much effort and planning. My most frequent performances are at church, and I've learned what and how much to eat for breakfast so I won't be too full during the first service or too hungry during the second one! When I perform at night (much less frequently), I plan exactly what to eat sev-eral days ahead. I make sure I have a solid breakfast and lunch, and then eat only a small, carefully-chosen snack before the performance. Before my recovery, nervousness and excitement would be a direct route to the refrigerator, so I'm especially careful on those days. I stick to my food plan, although I still have great difficulty delaying my dinner till late at night.

I'm embarrassed to admit it, but sometimes I'm more anxious about how I'm going to look on stage than how I'm going to sound. Overeating has caused me to spend a lot of time feeling bad about myself, and such feelings have had an impact on my confidence. Performing music means walking on and off stage, moving with the music, being in the spotlight. I've spent inordinate amounts of energy figuring out what to wear for concerts. Does this dress make me look fat? Is that outfit too dressy? Not dressy enough? Will people notice my stomach moving in and out as I breathe? As a woman, and particularly as a person with a lack of confidence in my looks, I used to find it nerve-racking to be the center of attention on stage. People came to hear my music, but in my mind, they were all looking at and evaluating my body. With recovery, maturity, and experience, I have come to love being on stage, and I now perform with confidence and joy, free from my old obsessive thoughts and fears.

> The practice of music can push every button you have, especially the one that puts yourself down. . . . Working musicians confess every variation on this theme. . . . We want to be beautiful and creative, and we continually refer to cultural models who are supposed to be. We do fear the failure of not living up to these standards of success. . . . This is a deep problem and I don't know the solution. But I do know that music can be learned only one way: by absorption in vibration. A mind immersed in the sound of sound does not have room for angry captions. . . . Zero in on the sweet sound of musical sound. Your self-nagger may seem all consuming and out of control, but musical tone has greater power than even that voice.
>
> —W. A. Mathieu, *The Listening Book*

I used to try to nurture myself with food, and instead I was self-destructive, losing touch with my musicality and creativity. Now I nurture myself with the things I really need: love, friendship, meditation and prayer, a good night's sleep, hugs, and music. Food used to keep me from enjoying life and music; now music feeds my soul and keeps me healthy and happy.

Music for the Love of It, December 1994

Tongue Depressed

Not long ago my dentist found an abnormal growth on the underside of my tongue, a body part I use for three of my favorite activities: talking, eating, and playing the flute. It's not an organ on which most flutists would want to have surgery! But surgery I did have, and while it was not pleasant, I was surprised to learn a lot about being a musician.

I couldn't play my flute for two weeks after the procedure. When I finally picked up my instrument and played some tentative notes, all I could manage were a few long tones for five minutes. The second day, I played long tones and slow, slurred scales for a quarter of an hour. My tone was terrible. A week passed before I could even look at a piece of legato music.

Over the next weeks, although I increased my practice time a little each day, my embouchure had lost muscle strength, and I didn't have the subtle inner control to which I'd been accustomed. I didn't hear improvement and became discouraged, but I kept practicing. When I went to my scheduled flute lesson, the flute was not taken out of its case. I taught my students, embarrassed by the sounds I made, and I kept practicing.

I shared my process with my flutist friends around the world on the online FLUTE List. Many of them wrote that I would recover and would become a better musician because of what I was going through. I didn't believe them.

People said that I was an inspiration to them, but I felt impatience with the slowness of the process. One woman wrote, "How do you do it? It's so hard to keep at it when you don't enjoy the sounds you're making."

I answered, "Two things motivate me to practice . . . One: I have two performances coming up. There is *nothing* like a performance to make me practice. I'm an amateur level player, so my tone is never what I *really* want, but I'm satisfied when I sound the best that I can sound, and I'm definitely not there. I'm practicing to get back to that point in time for the performances.

"Two: the way I see it, either I want to get my tone back, or I don't. Even if I practice, my tone may not come back, but chances are that it will; there is hope. If I don't practice, I have a guarantee that it won't. The *only* thing I can do is practice. It's no fun, and discouraging, but it's the path to get where I want to go. I hold my nose (not literally) and keep playing even though I can't stand what I hear. I just keep going."

I knew the exact moment when I declared myself officially recovered. At a lesson, I played an etude that I'd been working on. I thought my tone had improved, but I still didn't think it was good. My teacher's comment at the conclusion of the etude was, "Helen, I have never heard your tone sound better. That was just terrific. Your playing has reached a new level since your surgery." I went home and sheepishly wrote to my friends on the listserv that they had been right after all.

As I write this, I still cannot tackle double- or triple-tonguing, because it hurts to do so. With patience and the passage of time, my tongue will heal more and those skills will return. This process has been a test of my patience. I always have endless patience with my students and others, but not with myself.

I've learned that when I share my fear and discouragement with fellow musicians, they understand at a deep level what I'm going through, and they support me.

A man I'd never met sent me a flute CD, saying that there are many ways to become a better flutist without playing on the instrument. My pianist friend offered to take time off from work to take care of me. A woman in Scotland sent me a handwritten card. One of my 12-year-old students telephoned one morning the week after surgery. She wanted to know how I was doing and told me she missed me. After I thanked her from my heart, I asked to speak to her mother. She told me her mother wasn't at home. This child had called me unprompted. One man across the country wrote saying that because I was such a beautiful person, I could not help but make beautiful sounds again. Wow.

I can relate better, now, to my students who stop playing for awhile and then pick up their music-making again. I generated many ways to take a productive music lesson even though I couldn't play my instrument. For example, I spent one lesson listening to five recordings of the same piece and analyzing them with my teacher.

I was profoundly reminded about how precious it is to play and teach music. Because I do it every day, sometimes I take it for granted. The ability to make music and live a musical life is a gift from God, a privilege that few have, and the result of years of preparation. Such a blessing deserves my conscious awareness and deep gratitude every day.

I wouldn't recommend surgery on your tongue if you play a wind instrument. But if that becomes a necessity, look for the gifts. There are many.

Music for the Love of It, August 1997

Gifts of Music

esterday, I went to the hospital to visit a vibrant 40-ish friend, a singer, songwriter, and guitar player, who was hit by a car two weeks ago. She is paralyzed below the waist. I took my flute with me and asked her if she wanted me to play. She was most eager, saying that she didn't feel like being social anyway, so for about 40 minutes I played soothing music. She had her eyes closed and seemed happy and relaxed. When I left the hospital, I felt grateful that I know how to play this beautiful instrument and that I've been given the ability to give someone like my friend a gift of the spirit. Those 40 minutes were a better gift for her than anything I could have bought in a store. We didn't talk much before or after, but I left feeling that she and I had connected deeply; I felt our love for one another.

This experience prompted me to ask other musicians about ways they've given musical gifts. I posed the question to friends and on the Internet. Jim Cleere, who sings with an Iowa gospel group, related this story: "In the fall of 1992, our group was invited to sing for a nursing home. We went there on one of those cold snowy Iowa Sunday afternoons when you would just as soon be in front of the TV, sipping warm apple cider. We sang old hymns, and afterward each person smiled and expressed the tremendous meaning of each of our songs: this hymn was played at their wedding, that song was their husband's favorite . . . the power of music transformed these formerly useful, vital citizens who had simply become old. Like baking bread, it takes you back to your first memory of that smell—music transformed them, for a moment, into their younger selves. I hope that in the future, when I am wheeled into that room, another person or group is standing there ready to perform. And I hope that our contact will be as rewarding to them as mine was to me."

Randolph Case, the director of the Atlanta Center of Music for Healing and Transition, shared a personal story. "Our mountain dulcimer group came up with the idea of sharing our music with folks at a home for the profoundly retarded. The excited little group was made up of mostly beginning players, although two people thought that nothing 'amateurish' was suitable for a 'public performance.' But everyone did show up at the appointed hour. We made some mistakes and couldn't tell for certain that our music was getting through. We had just started our third song, 'Greensleeves,' when a young woman in the front row, who had been severely contorted, sat up and started to sing. She sang through the whole song—all the verses, right with us on pitch and tempo. After she finished, there wasn't a dry eye in the house, including the two who thought we weren't ready to play for anyone. The nurse told us later that this was the first intelligible sound she had ever heard from the young woman. We meant to share the gift of music with the people we played for. We didn't expect the gift we received."

Susan Dirks-Henry lives in Apple Valley, Minnesota. She plays her harp for sick and premature babies in the special care nursery. Each time a new baby is brought in, she composes a song especially for him or her, just as she imagines the angels did for us upon our births. One baby's family was so touched that they invited her to play at their baby's baptism.

Music accompanies us from birth to death. Mark Smith told me about the song he wrote for his mother who was dying of cancer. The song is about how precious life is, that there's nothing wrong with dying, and that all souls are connected even beyond death. "The cancer was making communication hard for her," Mark told me, "but she could hear fine. During my last visit to her, I played my guitar and sang the song for her and our family. We were all clearing our eyes and breathing deep, letting the feelings flow, releasing and yet maintaining concentration on the song as it took us through some kind of passage. Now, two years later, I'm still so glad that my Mom knew that we would miss her but that she was free to go. Whew! It was so intense that just telling about it brings it all back."

Ellen Zimmerli, who often plays her flute as a gift at weddings, tells of when two of her best friends performed at her wedding. "Donna played some Bach sonatas on flute and Jane sang 'Ave Maria.' The music was so beautiful. I was in tears during most of the ceremony. I believe that the music was one of my most beautiful gifts. It will last forever and take up no space on any cabinet, yet will always take a big space in my heart."

Peter Mason lives in Australia, is an amateur musician, and has a day job totally unrelated to music. Three of his co-workers asked him to teach them basic musicianship and to play the recorder, so he has a class for them at lunchtime every Monday. He charges them nothing, but he says, "It's a real buzz for me, and a thrilling new experience for them. It's my gift to them."

Barbara Duhl-Emswiler gave a surprise gift to her coworkers at her first company party. "We had the party at our CEO's home, a beautiful contemporary residence atop Seattle's Queen Anne Hill with views from Mt. Rainier to the islands in Puget Sound. Our office manager, who arranged the party, was secretive about the entertainment, saying it was a surprise. I got there early, set up my harp, and then just hung out as a guest until later. It was great fun to hear all the speculation about who this mystery harpist was going to be! And it was equally fun to see the reactions of my coworkers when they found out it was me! I hadn't worked there very long and most people didn't know I played."

Sonia Rosen of Ambler, Pennsylvania, related, "It was Christmas, and I was almost broke. I didn't know what to give my parents. My father had been learning the song 'Longer,' a love song by Dan Fogelberg. He loved it and often sang it to my mother. I play piano, so for more than two months I worked on that song, figuring out my own dynamics and putting all my feelings into it. I recorded it and decorated the cassette cover myself. I made a tape for each of my parents so that they could use the song to feel the love between them wherever they went. My parents said it was the best present they ever got."

Stephanie Wilson's family has a tradition of calling and singing "Happy Birthday" to whoever has a birthday, and sometimes Stephanie plays her trumpet over the phone instead. Ben Lewis, a 6-year-old from California, came up with the idea of having a bunch of friends bake cookies and give them to the neighbors while caroling. Catherine Proulx, of Quebec, said that in the eighth grade she played with her school band for a little girl who had cancer. The money was raised to make the little girl's dream come true: going to Disneyland. Ashima Khanna, age 11, plays her violin and harp at weddings and nursing homes in her home town of Ashland, Kentucky. When Gina Cox from Minnesota woke up on her 16th birthday, four of her girlfriends came into her room with their instruments—bassoon, flute, violin, and piccolo—and played "Happy Birthday" to wake her up. My own 10-year-old student, Christine Perry, played her flute for her grandparents' 50th wedding anniversary, lovingly decorated the sheet music with a special program on her computer, and framed it to present to them as a memento.

Sometimes the gift of music is given publicly, for charity. Calla Fireman, a Canadian flutist, played for five hours at a Cut-A-Thon sponsored by hairdressers who cut hair all night long, to help raise $2,000 for AIDS patients. Sometimes the gift is intimate, like the one from Stephen Duncan of Portales, New Mexico, who "has been known to have dinner with a special friend—flowers, candlelight, and cuddling her next to me as I play my Celtic harp just for her."

Tim Brimmer, a professor of music education and technology at Butler University in Indianapolis, sums it up wonderfully. "I sing John Denver songs to my wife, I sing lullabies to my children at bedtime, and soothing folk songs when they've been hurt. Music is a gift to be shared. I find great joy in giving the gift of song to people young and old. I have the joy of seeing the fruits of my labor spring up in the faces of newlyweds and church members. I have seen the tears of deepest passion pour down the cheeks of nuns in Germany while I was conducting liturgical music. I've seen Italian girls swoon while being serenaded by a barbershop quartet. I've seen proud parents burst into applause in response to their children's performance of difficult repertoire. I've seen human prejudice converted to respect during intense rehearsals, and I've seen respect turn into deep admiration during performances. Yes, music is a beautiful gift to give, and I'm a very happy person because of it."

Music for the Love of It, April 1996

Feeding Grandma J

So yesterday, I feed Grandma J her lunch—Grandma J isn't my grandma, but that's what everyone calls her, and I've known her for 30 years or so. I feed her in her room in the nursing home. I notice she's less alert than last week, but after her meal, she asks to be taken out onto the porch. So I put my flute, music, and stand on her lap and roll her outside in her wheelchair.

First I play the song she'd asked for, "My Happiness," which was her love song with her husband. I found that song for sale on eBay and brought along some books of the '30s and '40s, which I ordered and received in time to take for yesterday's visit.

So I'm sitting there on the porch with my flute in the 94-degree, horribly humid Carolina heat, playing this song, feeling rivulets of sweat dripping down my face and every other body part I own. I notice that Grandma J is sitting beside me dressed in not one, but two acrylic knit sweaters, and she has a heavy blanket over her legs. During this song, she closes her eyes, and I imagine, or guess, or wonder, whether she's communing with her dear Wesley, to whom she was married 72 years. But no—when I finish, I realize she's asleep. I sit still and quiet with her for about five minutes, and she wakes, saying, that was beautiful. I leaf through my '40s book and play more songs. I don't know most of them but sight-read them anyway, and I play the ones I do know, the ones from musicals.

About eight other elderly folks sit on the other end of the porch. I've heard about how, at different nursing homes, the various residents reacted enthusiastically when my friends played their flutes. I wondered if these people might get up and dance or something. Nope. These folks completely ignore me. A little later, a "young" man visiting his mother waves at me and says, "That was nice, thanks!" I'm too hot to do more than smile at him.

My flute swims all around my chin, and my back hurts from the uncomfortable position I sit in, in an attempt to sit close to Grandma J so she can hear the music with her poor ears. After a half hour or so, I stop playing and wheel her back to her (ahhhhh!) air-conditioned room. She wakes up long enough to thank me and say she loved the music. I tell her I'll be back again and play for her some more. I know that by the time her daughter comes for dinner, she'll have forgotten I was here.

When I call Grandma J's daughter to report in, she says that the doctors found a blood clot in her mother's leg the day before and that her condition is worsening. That's why she was less alert and sleepier.

It's likely that Grandma J won't be around for that much longer. She has 26 grandchildren and about 10 grown great-grandchildren. None of them knows how to play an instrument. I'll sit in the heat for her again, and bring her the music of her youth and of her beloved. Even with my days so full and busy, what could I possibly do that would be more important than that? How can I express, yet again and again and again, the gratitude for having the humble power to breathe music through the flute, to send music into the heart and soul of an angel almost ready to leave for the heaven world?

Tune In, Raleigh Area Flute Association Newsletter, September 2010

A Little Light Music

Victor Borge said, "Laughter is the shortest distance between two people." He was so right. I can't count the wonderful times I've had with my musical friends, sitting around a table, swapping jokes and funny stories. Something about laughing together makes you feel like family. This is a collection of some of my favorites, so pull up a chair and join us. "Three flutists went into a bar . . ."

A *New* What?

"Here, play those same tones on my flute," says Brooks, my flute teacher, handing me his solid gold, custom made, state-of-the-art instrument. I hold onto it for dear life and blow.

"Hmmm," says Brooks.

This little scene replayed itself many times during several years of lessons. Then, last October, after the part where I do the blowing, Brooks changed his line. "You need a new headjoint," he said.

I was so excited! My tone had developed enough that my old headjoint was holding me back and I would benefit from a new one. The headjoint, the top third of the flute into which the air is blown, creates about 70 percent of the tone quality of the flute. Although I have a superb instrument, today's headjoint technology is much more advanced than it was in 1965 when my flute was made. And this comment from my teacher was an objective measure of my improvement. Even the pesky, insecure little voice in my head couldn't argue with such objectivity or convince me that Brooks compliments my playing because he's "being nice."

I called my friend Pam to tell her I was getting a new headjoint. She sounded incredulous and asked, "Are you going to start smoking marijuana?"

I had a big concert the following month, so I decided to concentrate on the concert and order my new head (as many flutists refer to it) afterwards. Discipline suppressed eagerness, and I waited till the Monday after the concert to call Dana Sheridan of Boston, whom Brooks recommended as the best headjoint maker in the world. Dana said that normally he could send me a head to try within two weeks, but he was leaving the country on Saturday—for three months. Because I had already delayed my gratification, the next three months crept by very slowly. I started to be disgusted with my tone.

I told my friend Sandi how anxious and eager I was to get a new headjoint. She asked, "All this emotion over a new gasket in your car?"

Finally, Dana came back, and on a Thursday he sent me two headjoints to try, via Next Day Air. However, that "next day" there was a snowstorm in Louisville, where UPS does its thing, and the heads didn't get to me before my flute lesson on Friday. Brooks was leaving town the following week, and I needed his help to make this big decision. I cried in frustration in Brooks' studio. He astounded me by lending me his silver flute for the weekend, so that at least I could get used to playing on a Sheridan headjoint. I felt so honored that he trusted me in that way. In fact, I had a concert to play the next day, and in a fit of craziness I played the concert on his flute. No sane musician would play a concert on an unfamiliar instrument. But at this point, I was willing to live dangerously—anything not to have to listen to myself play on my old headjoint.

When the headjoints finally arrived, they didn't fit my flute. I sent them back to Dana with my old headjoint, so that he could adjust the new ones.

For insurance purposes, the lady at the UPS office asked for the contents and value of my package. "I'm shipping headjoints worth three thousand dollars," I stated. She didn't blink an eye. "Oh, yeah, I know about them fancy parts for motorcycles."

During all this flurry, Dana and I were on the phone with each other once or twice a day. About the time Brooks was due back, Dana was leaving for another six weeks, and I thought I would die if I had to wait much longer. So Dana and I discussed the logistics of every possible variation: if I liked one of the heads, then I could send it to him, and he'd send it back by Thursday; if I didn't like either one, would we have enough time for me to receive another one to try and then get it back to him for fitting before everyone left town? We laughed heartily about the bizarre predicament.

At the last second, the headjoint of my dreams arrived, and it fit my flute. All the aggravation had been worth it; the headjoint improved my tone beyond my grandest expectations.

I am grateful that during this process I had the support and assistance of my teacher, and that Dana Sheridan was so kind, accommodating, and understanding of my needs. Mostly I'm glad that I had such supportive and caring friends to listen to all the details of this story as it unfolded. When I told my friend Beth that I was getting a new headjoint, she asked with deep concern in her voice, "You mean like in your neck? Will you have to have surgery?"

Music for the Love of It, December 1993

Moments from a Flute Teacher's Journal

Most teachers could write a book about the unexpected and endearing ways their students and colleagues see the world. Here's a chapter from mine—an assortment of gems that I've shared in both stories and posts to the FLUTE List. (The real Janie, Kristen, Charlotte, Carolyn, Susie and Kevin will no doubt be relieved to see that their identities are concealed with pseudonyms.)

EXCUSES, EXCUSES

Probably most teachers have had students come in for their lesson and make an excuse for not having practiced that week.

Today one of my young girls came in and made her "confession" in the most succinct and adorable way I've ever heard.

Janie said, "I've lost my practiceness."

WHO KNEW?

I've been teaching 11-year-old Kristen for three years. She was motivated to practice during the first year, but the second and most of the third year have been difficult. She'd often come to lessons unprepared. I tried everything: charts, rewards, parental help, talking to her, you name it.

"Why aren't you practicing?"

"I dunno."

"What else can I do that would help you?"

"I dunno."

"Do you want to quit taking lessons?"

"No."

So I hung in there with her, although it was hard. The last few months, though, I noticed a big difference. She came prepared to lessons, her playing improved, etc.

"Have you been practicing more lately?"

"Yes."

"What stimulated this change?"

"I dunno."

Yesterday her mother attended the lesson. Her mother told me that now every night, she has to *force* (that was her word) Kristen to *stop* practicing so that she can do her homework.

I don't know why this change occurred—certainly nothing I did made it happen. But I'm glad I hung in there with her. This girl might have just fallen in love for the rest of her life.

AN IMPORTANT ANNOUNCEMENT

Charlotte is 10. She's a smart girl, but she doesn't talk much. Only with much coaxing does she answer questions about her day at school or her weekend activities. She rarely initiates any conversation.

Today, however, she uncharacteristically volunteered some information all by herself.

"I have lice," she announced.

Thank you very much for sharing that, Charlotte.

BRAVA

Today one of my adult students said this during her lesson:

"I'm not into performing for other people. I just want to play the flute for my own amazement."

RELAX, OLD TIMER

Yesterday I was finishing up a lesson with one of my adult beginners —I'll call her Carolyn. Carolyn has studied flute for only three months and will be participating in her first student recital next week. After I gave her some coaching about being on stage (smile, take your time, bow, etc.) she played through her simple recital piece, one of the easiest pieces in the first solo book, and then we ended the lesson.

Carolyn usually cleans her flute in the waiting room. The next student, Susie, was also out there, waiting her turn. Susie is a small child, about as tall as my kneecaps, and she is playing an entire concerto by memory as her recital piece.

Susie and Carolyn had this conversation, as I overheard it:

CAROLYN: Well, hi there, how are you?

SUSIE: Good! Are you playing in the recital?

CAROLYN: Yes. But I'm a beginner, it's just a simple piece.

SUSIE: Well, you have a lot of guts to go out there and play in front of an audience. That really takes courage.

CAROLYN: Yes, but I'm pretty nervous.

SUSIE: Well, you sound really good. I know you'll do real well. Just remember we've all been there. You're going to be just fine.

HARD DAY AT THE OFFICE

Ten-year-old Kevin comes into my studio for his lesson, throws himself on the couch, looks exhausted (partly true and partly pretense), and stares glassy-eyed into the distance.

"What's the matter, Kevin?" I ask him. "Did you have a hard day at the office?"

"Oh, man," he groans, "we had to cook all day in school today for our Thanksgiving feast tomorrow, and I'm so tired, and I still have lots of homework for tonight."

"I'm sorry you're having a hard day," I sympathize.

"Well, at least I'm here and not at track meet or Boy Scouts."

Curious, I ask, "Why is that?"

"Because flute lessons are more fun than track or Boy Scouts."

Flute lessons more fun than sports or scouts??? My day is made.

GULLIBLE PIANIST

On Friday night I'm rehearsing with my pianist. She turns to me and with great enthusiasm exclaims, "Helen! Your tongue sounds really good tonight! Everything seems so clear! Have you been doing something different?"

Being in a silly mood, I give her a true answer with a straight face, "Yes, I've been eating a lot of Weight Watchers Chocolate Fudge ice pops."

She looks at me quizzically. I devilishly keep on.

"Yes, the continued action of the tongue going in and out and up and down on the combined sweet flavor of chocolate and the perfect level of coldness develops an exquisitely fine articulation."

She says to me, deadly serious: "Is this a technique that a lot of flutists use?"

ANTS AND RABBITS AND FROGS — OH, MY!

Today one of my students, a sweet 8-year-old girl, brought her pet *snake* with her to her lesson to show me. This was a live snake, folks — a four-foot-long fat Columbian boa.

I'm not kidding. She brought the snake in a backpack, believe it or not. I didn't know whether to scream or to laugh. I did manage to get through the lesson, with the snake curled up in the backpack on my studio couch.

I've had kids bring hamsters, rabbits, frogs, ant farms, turtles, and sometimes even a live human baby brother or sister, but never a snake. Some people think that staying home and teaching flute all day is boring. Little do they know how exciting it really is.

SHE'S IN

Good morning, Brooks! That little 9-year-old girl you sent me a few weeks ago? She couldn't come for lessons in the early slots I had for younger kids who get out of school early. But with her long black braided hair, glasses sitting on the cutest face, and the clear, giant sound that came out of this tiny girl's flute, I was smitten. I made a spot for her. She had her first lesson yesterday. Thanks for another great referral.

My new student asked me, without inhibition, how old I was.

I asked her, "How old do you think I am?" And without a moment's hesitation, she yelled out, "TWENTY!" That's another reason I accepted her.

ESCAPE ARTIST

How to get out of an etude: bribery. Works every time.

Yesterday was my flute teacher's birthday, and as I do every year, I brought him a little gift when I went for my lesson today. I'd noticed that his leather key holder was tattered and torn, so I bought him a new one, in black leather, with shiny new key rings. He opened the wrapped box at the beginning of the lesson, and he seemed to like and appreciate the gift.

As the lesson proceeded, we came to the etude I'd been working on. Two weeks ago, I'd started working on it in single tongue. I usually enjoy etudes, but I hated this one. It was boring and tedious. I despaired when last week, my teacher assigned it to me again, this time in double tongue. I could see a pattern developing. Next week, triple tongue, then heaven knows what other torturous way he'd cook up to play this etude.

When I opened my book to the awful page, this popped out of my mouth without forethought: "By the way, that really wasn't a birthday present. It was a bribe. If you assign this etude to me again, I'm taking back the key holder."

My teacher's big, booming laugh filled the studio. We both chuckled as I started the long, mind-dulling exercise once again. When I got to the end, my teacher showed me where I had missed a note or two, and also pointed out a couple of printing errors. No comment on my articulation. Nothing about the evenness—or unevenness—of my rhythm. No correction of the movement of my embouchure. Silence.

My teacher flipped the page, assigning me the next etude, saying, "I want to keep my key holder."

Try it. Works every time.

FELIX WHO?

I wish to announce that there has been a major change regarding the information we have about a well-known composer of the 19th century who has written music for the flute.

On Friday, October 8, 2004, just two days ago, I questioned a world expert on the study repertoire of the week, just before he was about to embark on the performance of such repertoire. I inquired about the name of the composer of the piece in question, "On Wings of Song." The composer's name was written clearly on the page.

With great firmness, dignity, and confidence, due to his many years (8) of listening to music since he was born, and the specific study of music and the recorder for one and a half grueling years, he answered:

Felix Mendelonius.

Ladies and Gentlemen, please correct your manuscripts herewith.

WAY COOL!

It's Saturday afternoon. The phone rings, and I hear the panic-stricken voice of my 13-year-old student, Eric: "Helen, do you have a tuner?" I say that I do. "Oh, thank God, oh, that's so great. Can I borrow it?"

I ask him what he wants to use it for. He says he has to do a science experiment that's due on Monday. He received the assignment in December but has left it to the last minute. I tell him that he can use my tuner. He agrees to do his experiment at my house because it will only take a half hour or so, and because I'm a little wary of him taking my tuner for a few days.

Eric arrives. I give him my tuner and leave him to his own devices. A short while later I get thirsty. I go to get some juice, and there on the refrigerator shelf, carefully nestled on top of a folded towel, are the three parts of Eric's flute.

"MY GOD, ERIC, WHADDAYA DOING???"

He says he is cooling the flute so that he can test the effect of temperature changes on pitch. He proudly explains that as soon as the flute comes out of the refrigerator, he will place it in the electric heating pad he brought from home so that he can contrast the effect of heat on the pitch of his instrument.

"DON'T YOU KNOW THAT THIS IS NOT A GOOD THING FOR YOUR FLUTE???"

Well, yeah, he says. He knows. But he's got to get an experiment done by Monday, and besides, it's only for a few minutes.

Eric leaves, happy and grateful. I think, "If I tell this story on the FLUTE List, they'll think I made it up." I didn't, I swear.

On the Menu Tonight

I had an exceptionally busy day yesterday and, to my dismay, only got in about 10 minutes of practice. Then I got an idea that I had never thought of before.

Freddy and I had plans to have dinner at our friend's house. The friend, Sunil, had invited us and another couple, but at the last minute the others couldn't come. So it would just be Sunil, a longtime good friend, and us. The plan was for Sunil, a *fabulous* cook, to give Freddy a cooking lesson in the absolutely delicious Indian food he had learned to cook as a boy growing up in India. Freddy loves to cook and has been aspiring to increase his repertoire of Indian recipes.

As we got ready to leave the house, I announced to Freddy, "I'm going to take my flute and play some pre-dinner cooking music for you, and get some practice time in." Freddy's immediate reaction was, "Oh, what a great idea! We'll love it!" Then, a minute later, he did a double-take and looked at me in horror. "You're not going to play those *scales*, are you?" I assured him that I wouldn't.

So I stood in Sunil's living room, who was thrilled to turn off his CD in favor of live music, and played the pieces I'm working on. After a while, the guys turned on the above-the-stove fan, which made some noise, and I could hear they were deeply engrossed in talking about tamarind sauce and cumin seeds and whatever, so I even snuck in my etude. I played for about an hour, repeating some sections that I wasn't pleased with. It wasn't the kind of concentrated practice I normally do, but at least I played for an hour in a day that I might not have otherwise.

When we sat down to dinner, they told me that Sunil has one of those key chains that beep when you whistle, so that you can find your keys. They said my flute-playing kept setting it off and they had to hide it in a drawer. They expressed appreciation for my music. Then we had an absolutely scrumptious Indian dinner. Life doesn't get much better than this!

FLUTE List, April 26, 1997

A Musical Name Game

A few months ago, my husband, a physician, showed me a funny article about doctors whose names relate to their profession, as in Needle, Fix, Cure, Rash, Knee, Ache, and others. I began to wonder whether musicians had equally humorous names, so I spent many hours in the University of North Carolina Music Library pouring over *Who's Who in American Music* and other similar sources.

Many musicians share names with instruments, such as Horn, Bell, Viola, Fyfe, Celli, Lutes, Bass. I also found a composer named Oboe, a percussionist named Kettle, a flutist named Toote, organists named Piper and Hammond, and my favorite: a double bass player named Low.

Some people have names that refer to parts of instruments, like Reed, the most common; others are Key, Stringer, Bridge, Spring, Bowes, and Hammer. Some names suggest the body parts used to play the instruments, such as Lipp and Hand. Occasionally, a musician's name describes what one of those body parts might do while performing, such as Shake, Trembly, Huff, Stiffin, or Blose, and for the determined, Blomore.

Many musicians share the name of a great composer, such as Grieg, Mahler, Copeland, Bach, Wagner, Weber, Berg, Gluck, Leclair, McDowell, Praetorius, and Mancini. Some come pretty close, like Hoffman, Hayden, Handelsman, Khatchadourian, Kohler, Martineau, and Mendelson.

From a theoretical perspective, a number of people in the music field are named Sharp, Sharper, and Sharpley, while others are named Flatt or Flatau. I didn't see any Naturals. There is a musicologist in this country named Minor, and a pianist is named Major. Others are named Register, Barr, Key, Acord, Toney, Melody, Thieme, Toone, and Tuneberg. There is a piano teacher named Triplett.

In a timely fashion, there is a flutist named Tempa, a bassoonist named Quick, a cellist named Hasty, a music appreciation teacher named Fast, pianists Early and Lively, and flutists Hurry and Speed. The "fast" names far outnumbered the "slow" ones, although I did find a pianist named Wait and a music theory historian named Grave. Luckily, some musicians are right on the beat, with names like Beaty, Counts, and Goodspeed.

Dynamically speaking, there is a composer named Crescendo, a clarinetist named Biggers, and my favorite, a tuba player named Louder. I couldn't find any piano players named Piano. I located musicians whose names tell about forms and styles of music: Minuetta, Ode, Gregorian, Grosso (a specialist in the aesthetics of music), Grossi, Cannon, Rapp, Bopp, March, Rounds, Siciliano, Song, Carol, Gloria, Waltz, and even a Brandenburg. Opera is represented by musicians named Arias, Singer, and Sung (one of the Singers' first names is Carol), a horn player named Faust, a musical instrument curator named Voice, and (possibly) a trombone player named Schmalz. Lots of women musicians share names with heroines of opera or ballet, such as Mimi, Giselle, Lucia, Lauretta, Norma, and Carmen.

A few lucky musicians' names remind them of the importance of regular practice, such as Daily, a flutist, and pianists Daley and Weekly. There is a band leader named Drill. Unfortunately, one brass musician is named Cancel. I hope he's not on a concert tour.

When you have Heard (a violinist) wonderful music, you probably Clapp (a violinist and an organist) or call out Bravo (a bassoonist, a pianist) or do a little unabashed Yelin (a eurhythmics instructor). You admire the Maestre (a flutist) or the Starr (a pianist) of the evening. Most people love to watch a musician perform who is a real Hamm (there are lots of Hamms in the music business). Some of you might hear these musicians on Broadway (a pianist) or in Vienna (a pianist), and if you get carried away, might want to go to the backstage of the concert Hall (dozens) to Kiss (a pianist) the performer. By the way, one of the folks named Hall is a sound and acoustics technologist.

Speaking of kissing, I saw two musicians listed that you might want to hire for your next wedding. The harpist's name is Bride, and the organist's name is Groom. And don't forget Love and Ring.

I was most fascinated by names that expressed the feelings evoked by listening to or performing music, such as Joy and Gay. I found two brass players named Jolly, a mandolin player named Gladd, and an organist named Raver. I was amused to find a viola player named Bliss, a violinist named Nice, and pianists named Merrie and Loving.

Perhaps the most confident performers are the violinist and pianist named Shure, the pianist named Smart, or the two trumpet players named Best. If you play poorly, your music sounds like Noyes (a pianist) to your ears. There is a director of an orchestra named Pitts. If you were a flutist named Blank, you might forget your music; however, you could call on a music therapist named Memory. If the flutist named Fears gets too nervous to perform, she ought to team up with another flutist named Courage. The ones with the right idea are those with positive names, such as Good, Allgood, Aregood, and especially Goodenough.

For me, music is a path of growth I've traveled on all my life, which may be true for the flutist named Journey. Even I have a musical name, Spielman, which means "player" in German. I also found a director of a choral group named Batty and a trombone player named Blind, both of which I am, after writing this article.

Music for the Love of It, August 1993

Notes on the Internet

We take the Internet for granted now. But when I began teaching flute in 1990, I was alone in my own small world—just my students and me in my Chapel Hill studio. Then came the FLUTE List, and my professional life changed forever. The Internet connected me to the whole world of music. Suddenly, I could talk to thousands of colleagues who cared about what I cared about, who faced the same challenges and applauded the same victories. In these chatty, give-and-take Internet conversations, I still hear their thoughts and advice, still feel their passion and support. And I continue to thank them for making me a better teacher and flutist.

Skid Marks on the Internet

When I first got a new computer a year ago, I subscribed to FLUTE, the Internet mailing list for folks interested in the flute. The experience started slowly because the list was small, only a handful of messages were posted daily, and I had a modem of only 2,400 baud. After a few months at such limited speed, I got a 28,800 baud modem, a birthday gift from my husband. My faster modem came in handy as FLUTE grew to generate 20 to 30 messages a day. When I excitedly mentioned my new modem on a post, I received a reply from a flutist in Seattle who said, "Congratulations on your new faster modem. Don't leave skid marks on the Internet." I ignored his advice and happily began speeding through cyberspace.

I became aware of what an enormous music resource the Net could be when I first used it to search for music. I wanted to play *Pastorale Suite* by Gunnard de Frumerie, a Swedish composer, after I heard this charming piece on a CD. It was out of print and not available in the music libraries. I typed out a request and sent it into the ethers, and three days later received a response from a man in Sweden. He had the music and mailed it to me at his own expense.

By reading FLUTE and participating in the discussions, I've learned about new pieces of music to play, wonderful books to read, and great CDs to listen to. But the most meaningful part has been the friendships I've developed with people all over the world who share my passion for the flute. This was brought home to me powerfully last month when my first big solo recital was to have taken place. The week before the scheduled date, I asked my online fellow flutists for support, and I received almost forty email messages filled with good wishes, encouragement, positive thoughts, and caring. When the recital was canceled because of a big snowstorm, I received over thirty more messages of sympathy, empathy, shared sorrow, enthusiastic support for re-scheduling, and most importantly, love. I was overwhelmed, not only with the size but also with the depth of such a response.

Last summer at the convention of the National Flute Association, a few of us from FLUTE had dinner together so that we could meet face-to-face. Our group of ten was diverse, including the principal flutist of the New York City Opera, a composer, a young couple from The Netherlands, and several amateurs and teachers.

When my husband and I went to England last spring to celebrate our 20th wedding anniversary, one of the FLUTE folks, a flute maker who lives outside of London, traveled into the city to the British Museum to meet me. We sat on a bench outside the museum and chatted for an hour. I was delighted that a stranger would go so far out of his way to make my acquaintance.

This year, when I traveled to South Africa to visit my cousins, I met a woman from FLUTE who had asked me to bring her some music that was unavailable in her country. She drove from her home in Pretoria to Johannesburg where I was staying, and I made yet another friend and learned about flute activities in a country very different from mine.

A woman on FLUTE recently moved to my town, and we made plans to get together for coffee. I sat in the restaurant, waiting for her, and thought, "This is how it must feel to go on a blind date!" We managed to find each other and had a lovely conversation. We've kept in touch through email, and she has begun to study with my teacher.

One day I logged on and froze, staring at my screen in utter surprise, delight, disbelief, and amazement. James Galway—James Galway!—had sent me an email. I had met him briefly a year ago, but I didn't think he'd remember who I was, yet his message indicated that he knew exactly who I was and was initiating a conversation! We have been writing to each other ever since. I've come to know him as a warm, caring, generous person. Although I'm honored to have a friendship with someone of his fame, email has given me the gift of getting past the glamour to know him as the truly dear human being he is.

In my pre-email days, when I'd occasionally wake up in the middle of the night with insomnia, I'd read a book till I could fall back to sleep. Nowadays, if I'm up at 3 A.M., I'm at my computer. My husband teases me about how much time I spend on the Net, and he is amused by how excited I get about some of the topics of conversation or the jokes FLUTE members fling across the globe. What is not so obvious to an outsider, though, is how this experience contributes to my life as a musician. On a daily basis, I learn and grow. I'm stimulated by new ideas and am exposed to a wide variety of philosophies about teaching and making music. I find added incentive to practice when I regularly connect with others who practice diligently. I see an immense span of different people, as young as 11 or as old as 80, in Africa and Japan and Europe and Australia. Some have played flute their whole lives and are at the top of their profession; others are beginners—and I feel connected to them all through our common interest. There are lists for harpists, tuba players, bagpipers, and probably every musical instrument in existence.

While the process of making music itself remains timeless through the ages, the way that musicians meet, share ideas, and interrelate has been forever revolutionized. I'm delighted to participate in these exciting times. If I leave behind a few skid marks, I'm OK with that.

Music for the Love of It, June 1996
Reprinted in *Pan*, Journal of the British Flute
Society, Summer 1996

Here are just a few of the memorable Internet exchanges that have enriched my life in music, as a teacher and a performer and a friend. I have edited them for spelling and punctuation, but otherwise I have let them be their casual, chatty selves, triple exclamation points and all.

Re: A Sweet Flute Memory
Date: Nov. 22, 1996

When I was in my 20s I played in the Augusta Symphony Orchestra (Augusta, Georgia). We were rehearsing *Scheherazade** and in one of the movements, after many bars of rest, there is a short but wonderful 2nd flute solo. I occasionally came in on the wrong beat, or missed a note, or worst of all, didn't play staccato enough for the conductor.

He had this thing about staccato notes being *really* short. He had been a French horn player with the Chicago Symphony for many years. He used to scream and yell at me, but I didn't take it personally, because he screamed and yelled at everyone. Sometimes individuals, sometimes entire sections.

Anyway, the night of the performance, I started my solo at exactly the right beat, I was in tune, I played beautifully, my flute sounds soared over the orchestra, and those staccato notes were the shortest ever played on planet Earth.

When I looked up, the maestro was conducting away, but an incredible smile lit up his face—a smile of total satisfaction and pleasure. Even though he never made eye contact with me, that smile was for me. Or for my music, I should say. He continued to smile for several minutes more.

I will never forget that moment. It was my last performance with that

---

*Scheherazade, Op. 35 by Nikolai Rimsky-Korsakov.

orchestra before I moved to North Carolina. The warm glow is still in the memory of my soul, even 20 years later.

Helen

Re: Teaching Beginners
Date: Dec. 7, 1998
A FLUTE List writer had commented that beginners don't need to have real performance experiences until they've mastered the fundamentals . . .

I disagree with you on this. Performance situations are just as real and important and instructive with beginners as they are with more advanced students. I don't understand why you would keep beginners away from performing. This is the very time when they can learn the joy of sharing music, get their first chance at developing stage presence, and participate in a musical event by *contributing* to it, not just listening.

I think you do a serious disservice to all students by barring beginners from performance. The most likely place a beginner would perform is at a student recital. By not having beginners perform, the advanced students would lose out, too, because the beginners remind us all how far we've come, how difficult it is to play this instrument, and how privileged we are to be in the presence of children who have the courage and eagerness to show what they've learned, even if they haven't learned all the basics.

At what point would you say beginners should perform? Where is your arbitrary line—the line that says, yes, this beginner has learned the basic things and can now perform? I say that kind of attitude can cause a lot of problems for students.

My students' recital was yesterday. I had three children performing who are, by anyone's standards, absolute beginners. They each played pieces that contained only four notes, none more complex than a quarter note. Two had decent beginner tones; one had a tone that was so tiny you could barely hear her. But they played, participated, got nervous, joined our group support activity, received applause and compliments and award certificates, and learned more than I can write in this post.

Helen

Re: Bored With Classical

Date: Nov. 12, 2007

A FLUTE List writer had confessed to being a flutist who is bored to tears by classical music . . .

This is a sad confession, but hope is out there.

I had a 9-year-old boy start flute lessons with me last year who simply loved classical music before he began any kind of musical training. He listens to it all the time. It's his musical style of choice. He's 10 now, and does not (yet!) play musically. But every week, as I assign him an array of exercises, etudes, pieces, duets, etc., he comes back and says, "I liked this one the best." And without fail, he will have picked out the one work that has true musical value.

I want to—I have to—believe that classical music is alive and is a living form. It's not better or worse than any other kind of music, but it's alive in the hearts of some of our youngest, because my student can't be the only one.

Once again, here is an important principle: What we feed, grows. Let us continue to feed our young children, and let us continue to feed ourselves with the kind of music we love.

Helen

Re: Atonal By Choice?

Date: Oct. 7, 2003

Tod Brody posted:

It's very easy to limit oneself by holding onto an opinion, i.e. "I dislike (atonal) (minimalist) (spectral) (dissonant) (Chopin's) music." I've learned, when hearing something new and different, to resist reaching for an opinion. My opinion won't help me to true understanding, but could very well create a barrier. I just try to let the music happen to me, let it reach me on its own terms. When we hear a foreign language spoken, one with which we are not familiar, all we can hear are the sounds; the meanings they convey are not revealed to us, at least not at first. Over time and repeated exposure, the vocabulary, grammar, and syntax begin to reveal meaning.

I think what Tod wrote in this post a few days ago is one of the most meaningful statements I've ever read on FLUTE List. Not only was the content of great importance, but the intelligence, clarity, and conciseness with which it was stated had great impact on me. In fact, if I could have your permission, Tod, I'd like to print this out and post it on my studio bulletin board.

I'm a person who in my younger years enjoyed only a narrow variety of music, both to listen to (as in symphonic works) and to play on my flute. During my high school years, I was given some 20th-century works to study. But the way they were presented to me, I didn't understand them and therefore didn't like them. I was a good little flute student, and practiced them, but they had no meaning or beauty for me. It wasn't until later—through new teachers, listening to recordings, going to concerts—that I heard these pieces differently. And then I fell deeply in love with them, hardly understanding how I could have disliked them before.

Now, as a teacher, I make sure my students are exposed to a variety of styles and periods of music in understandable and enjoyable ways. But occasionally I have a young student like Patti (not her real name), an extremely talented, very advanced high school flute player, who is *adamant* about liking only Baroque and Classical literature, with an occasional foray into Romantic music, but not too often.

About three weeks ago—and this is another reason why I found Tod's statement timely for me—this student (who does not want to major in flute) and I conversed via email about her recital piece. I let my students choose pretty much anything they want to play for our student recitals, and she chose a Classical piece, and told me again she never wanted to play modern music. Here is an excerpt of what I wrote to her:

"I fully and completely want my students to play the kind of music they enjoy, and I am glad to see that you have definite ideas on what you like and don't like. My goal is not to "make" you like any certain kinds of music. However, as your teacher, I do feel that it's an important part of my job to introduce you to a variety of styles of the flute repertoire.

"If you left my studio at the end of your senior year having played primarily Baroque and Classical music, I'd feel that I did a crummy job in that aspect of your instruction, and I'm almost certain that if you continued your flute playing beyond high school—either seriously through lessons, or as a music minor, or even as a serious amateur player—you'd eventually come to feel the same way. I don't expect you to agree with me about that now, or to even fully understand it, but I do ask that you trust me enough to believe that I'm telling you the best truth that I know.

"I feel it's important for you to learn a few (not all) of the Romantic French flute pieces, which are considered almost like the meat and potatoes of the flute literature. If you learned only one a year—say, for example, the Taffanel, the Gaubert, and the Enesco–that would be satisfactory. I do feel it is important for you to learn several 20th-century works. Last spring you and I agreed that you would learn some contemporary pieces. I don't expect you to like it as much as you love Baroque. But I do expect you to keep your commitment to study a piece this fall.

"I want you to become a relatively well-rounded flute player while you're in my studio, otherwise I'd feel as though we were not doing justice to your efforts, your talent, or your growth potential as a musician. You need to have the exposure, Patti. You don't have to like it. But you need to experience it as you learn during this stage of growth. That is my opinion as your teacher who loves you and wants to be the best teacher for you that I can be.

"Quite honestly, there is some contemporary music that I don't like either. But there is some that is pretty nice, and some that is gorgeous. My advice to you (even though you didn't ask for it) is to try to keep an open mind, because you may expand your love of music in ways that you never thought would ever be possible.

"If you don't like a piece, tell me. Don't ever say you like a piece when you don't, just to please me. I want your honesty, just as I give you mine. Let's work through your repertoire choices together during these next years in a way that will be a good balance all around."

After this discussion, I gave Patti a Rampal CD of 20th-century sonatas, and she came back the following week and said, "Well, there actually is one modern piece I really like!"

It was the Poulenc.*

So I felt very triumphant because that's a start. And once she studies that—and knowing her, she'll learn to love it rather than like it—she'll find another one she likes. Just think! Two whole pieces . . . and you know the rest.

Developing an open mind to flute music, to music in general, to everything that exists—well, that would make this world a different place, wouldn't it? Music is a great place to start.

Helen

*"Sonata for Flute and Piano" by Francis Poulenc.

Re: Do I Really Need a Degree?
Date: Feb. 1999
Phyllis Louke posted:
   Many flute majors at my university who graduated with flute degrees haven't had their flutes out of their cases in 20 years . . .

Phyllis, this is a powerful statement—and a true one at that! Like you, I know many people who started out getting degrees in music and who now never play. There's nothing *bad* about that—people make changes in their lives for many reasons (as I did).

I think it's important for our young people to know that growing up to be an adult amateur musician is a wonderful thing to aspire to. They listen to CDs or attend a concert and think that the pro world is all that's available. As a teacher, I try to open their eyes to all the opportunities and joys that can await them in music even if they choose a different career path.

I never wanted to be a professional musician. And here I am, *two* careers later, still with no degree in music. But I perform regularly, I have a large, successful teaching studio, I write and speak on flute-related topics at the international level, and my life is pretty much involved with music from morning till night. I share that not to brag, but to show that it's *possible* (sometimes, literally, I still have trouble believing it myself).

Last Sunday afternoon, I went to listen to a small gathering of chamber music players. Various small groups performed for each other—a flute, violin, piano trio, a cello and piano duo, even a clarinet and Music Minus One cassette duo! Of the ones I knew, one was a math professor, one a physician, two computer people, one retired woman, one public health professional, and one emergency relief worker. None of them had a degree in music, but the enthusiasm for playing—and listening—to the music was unmistakable.

So to the person who asked the question in the subject line: Getting a degree in music is great if that's what you want, but you most definitely don't *need* a degree in music to continue to play and be involved in music for the rest of your life.

Helen

Re: Perfect Recital
Date: May 20, 2001
Leslie Skolnik posted:
    If you were creating what you think would be the perfect flute recital, what would it be?

Whatever would fill the flutist's heart and soul with joy and fulfillment.
                                     Helen

Re: Following Their Own Advice
Date: Nov. 14, 2000
Jean B. Hayes posted:
    Do other teachers have trouble following their own advice?

Hello, Jean. You have an amazing capacity to ask timely questions. Here's a story—a true story—that happened recently. I've been meaning to tell FLUTE List about it, but have gotten too busy, until your question stimulated me to write.

Two weeks ago, I walked into my flute lesson, ready to pop with frustration. "I've been working on these runs in this piece for four months," I told my teacher in a less-than-calm voice. "I can often get them at home, but I know, I just know they're not going to come out smooth and even and clear and clean next week when I perform them. I'm sick of working so hard and then having my notes be sloppy. And don't tell me to practice six hours a day. I don't have that kind of time and even if I did, I wouldn't practice that long. Just don't tell me that, because I'm not going to do it," I said, glaring at him and waiting for him to give me some impossible assignment to fix the problem.

Instead, he just stood there calmly, leaning against the piano, arms and legs casually crossed, eyes looking at me attentively, kindly, patiently waiting for me to be done with my tirade. (He's been my teacher for 11 years and knows me very well.) When I finally stopped ranting, he looked right into my eyes and asked, "Helen, do you believe in imagery?"

"What do you mean, do I believe in it?" I retorted. "Didn't I just tell you last week how I've been working with my little student on stage fright using visualization techniques? Of course I believe in it."

"Yes," he said, "but do you believe in it for you? It sounds to me as though you've talked yourself into thinking that you can't do this run. And if that's what you think, you're right, you'll never do it. You don't need to practice six hours a day. You need to see yourself succeeding, you need to find the inner confidence that knows that you can do this. This is not about your fingers, it's about your self-image."

His words rang true and hit me like a ton of bricks. I do spend a lot of time and energy helping my students with positive self-talk, visual imagery and confidence, but I have gotten sloppy about using those techniques for myself. I felt kind of sheepish, but also grateful that I have a teacher who can see things about me that I can't, and who's willing to be straight and honest in his feedback.

I went home and visualized. I thought about a feeling I've often felt in my life, a sort of inner knowingness that I can do whatever I set my mind to do. I tried to pair that feeling with playing that run. I saw a movie in my mind's eye of myself getting on that stage and allowing that difficult run to soar with grace and perfection.

Wouldn't you know, only a week later I performed that piece, and I *nailed* the run. I was so delighted, and I felt so satisfied.

So, to answer your question, Jean: yes, I often have trouble following my own advice. It's real easy to have all the answers for everyone else, but it takes humility and sometimes painful self-honesty to find them for myself.

Helen

Re: A Sighting in Cyberia
Date: Sept. 23, 1996

Within a five-minute walk from the flat we rented in London there's this Internet café called Cyberia. I went there several times but was frustrated because the connection was poor. I had wanted to write to FLUTE List from there, but just barely managed to get out a few tiny emails. Anyway, on my 4th visit, it was so bad that I decided not to go back anymore.

I decided to log off, and I was sitting there in front of the screen, waiting for it to s-l-o-w-l-y do its thing. I got bored and stared through the window. This café is on a small, non-descript side street. Nothing much to look at. Then I see a car, and about to get into the car is James Galway.

OK, Helen, you're daydreaming. I WAKE UP. It IS Jimmy, our very own Jimmy!!!

I leave the computer, my purse, everything, and DASH out into the street, totally freaked out and amazed and yelling, "Jimmy! Jimmy!" and he sees me and is totally surprised and we give each other a big hug.

"What are you doing here?" I asked. He explained that he was recording his next CD in the building next to the café (which didn't have a sign on it). I knew he was going to be in London because he had played that weekend at the Proms concert (a famous BBC concert series in London), but we couldn't attend.

"This is amazing," he kept saying. "What are you doing here?" he asked. I pointed to the Internet café. "I've never seen one, let's go in." He put a briefcase, which I presumed contained his flutes, in the car and asked the driver to wait. We went into the café and I showed him the screen where it STILL wasn't doing anything. We talked for a few minutes, and then he had to go.

What were the chances of two FLUTE List members running into each other, one from America, one from Switzerland, in the middle of a huge city like London? I only know that it was the most exciting thing about my whole trip!! Big hug to all of you,

Helen

Re: Convention Thoughts 2003
Date: Aug. 19, 2003
Patricia George had commented, regarding a flute concerto performed at the National Flute Association Convention, "there certainly were scary/awkward moments with the orchestra the entire night. The wonderful flute playing carried the evening. However, (the orchestra) made the evening more difficult for the solo performers. I suppose most of us have lived evenings like that, though. You just do your best."

Thank you, Patricia, for your keen observations, as always. There were obviously problems with the orchestra that evening, as well as during the rehearsal at which I was present. I agree that the soloists did an admirable job of performing well despite difficulties with the ensemble. I also observed some interactions that impressed me a lot, that were very considerate, professional, and kind, even under stress, among the various performers. Playing with perfect rehearsal conditions and fabulous performing scenarios is hard enough, but to do it under adverse conditions is the mark of a true professional.

This reminds me of the recent win by cyclist Lance Armstrong at the Tour de France. The previous four years, he won this three-week-long race seemingly effortlessly. This year, he had to fight for every second, overcoming a fall off his bike, flu, injury, dehydration, and all kinds of other difficulties. I read a wonderful editorial in *Sports Illustrated* that said, "this was Armstrong's great, great win, in that he still wound up best even at his worst . . . This was the year Armstrong beat them aching, beat them dumb, beat them unlucky."

If a flutist can still play so very beautifully, keep the music together, enthrall the audience, not lose his or her cool because of strange things going on in the orchestra, that's the mark of a "champion" flutist. I think we saw a few champion flutists last week.

Helen

Re: Inspiration
Date: Apr. 5, 1997
Kathleen Herb posted:

I need some teaching hints to inspire (students) to keep on with their music. What do all you experienced music and band teachers do to generate enthusiasm?

Be enthusiastic myself.

Helen

Re: Just an Amateur? Yes!
Date: Apr. 2, 1999
Someone posted:
Well, I didn't want to say anything since I'm just an amateur.

I'd like to re-introduce a topic that we've discussed before on the list, but that I feel is worth exploring again. And again . . . :)

Being an amateur musician is worthy of dignity and respect. Those of us, like myself, who are amateur players deserve to be looked upon as valued members of the world of music, but even more importantly, we deserve to think of ourselves as real and true musicians who have a great deal to offer to the world, and more specifically, to offer to our FLUTE list.

For many years, I felt insecure, confused—that I didn't really belong in the music world. It took several years to find myself as a musician, and what a relief it was to finally come to the understanding that being an amateur player is a vital, life-enhancing, dignified, intelligent, and joyous way to be a musician, in and of itself. It is *not* a "lesser form" of a professional player.

I'm happy to be an amateur flutist, and I'm proud of it, too! While I admire and deeply respect the many professional flutists I know—and long to sound as good as they do—I know that I would not have been happy putting in the long hours and years of practice to attain that level of playing. And I know that I don't have the talent to have achieved that, even if I'd put in the time. I've accepted that aspect of myself and know that the path I've taken in life has been the right one for me.

So, when I see someone say, "I'm just an amateur," I feel compelled to point out that we don't need to subtly put ourselves down, or perceive ourselves as not being good enough to contribute to discussions, or play in concerts, or give musical opinions, or anything else that we choose to do.

"The joy we derive from making music as amateurs is sometimes more like finding a single wildflower in the woods than like strolling through an extravagant formal garden in full bloom."—Stephanie Judy, *Making Music for the Joy of It.*

I'm grateful to have found my wildflower. Have you found yours?

Helen

Re: Grand Entrance
Date: Oct. 9, 1999
A FLUTE List writer had posed an interesting question for students: What do you find most helpful when you enter your teacher's studio?

My teacher's warm smile, his hearty hello, and a welcoming hug.

Helen

Re: Recordings Revisited
Date: Nov. 8, 1996
A comment had noted the value of diverse musical contributions and encouraged us to value our personal musical language and vision, no matter how large the audience might be. This wise musician advised that we should never let the talents or accomplishments of other performers inhibit our own sense of musical self-worth.

This was a powerful post that contained deep truth. And I want to take it even a step further, and say that even those musicians (flutists and others) who haven't reached a high level of competency have enormous value and are making important contributions to the world. To me, music is light and beauty, peace and joy. It's my belief that *every* time *anyone* plays music from their heart, they are sending vibrations of beauty into the world. And every bit of beauty makes less room for the sorrow and suffering and darkness to exist.

I have an adult student who used to constantly compare herself to James Galway and made herself miserable. One day I said to her, "You know, you'll never sound like Galway, no matter how hard or how much you practice. You'll always sound like Jane, because that's who you are. And Jane's music is just as beautiful and valuable and important as anyone else's."

The other day she told me that that statement was a turning point for her in learning to value and appreciate the beauty of her own music. I've made her a copy of the above post, and will give copies to my other adult students as well.

In my studio, I have a poster that says:

"The forest would be very quiet if only the best birds sang."

Helen

Re: Leaving Students
Date: May 20, 1996
Edwin Lacy posted:
Emotional bonds are developed (when teaching students), but I have long thought that in many instances, the music world would be better off if we could keep these relationships on a more professional level, with somewhat less emotional investment in the personalities of our students/teachers.

As you say, there are many different styles of teaching and relating to students. This is certainly true, and I respect the view you share above. But I do disagree with it for myself.

I believe that the world encourages us to keep our distance from people in too many ways. I think we need each other very much, and we are all deeply connected at our essence. Having one-on-one relationships with flute students gives me the opportunity to have an intimate bond with someone else. All of us, and especially children, need love and caring and attention and validation. I think teaching music is an opportunity to extend those things to our students. They don't get it in too many places in today's society. Too many other relationships have become "professional," and not enough, in my opinion, are deep and real and close.

This (emotional bond) can also lead to various kinds of excesses. I have observed a number of instances where teachers' methods caused their students to develop an excessive degree of emotional and psychological dependence on them. This has almost invariably led, eventually, to a potentially damaging situation when, for whatever reason, those bonds have to be severed.

I'd be interested to hear what you mean when you say "excesses." Do you mean an excess of love? I don't think there is such a thing. Do you mean an excess of caring and attention and effort? I don't think there is such a thing. Of course, teachers should teach and encourage and develop independence in their students—I certainly agree with you on that. But what damaging situation exists when bonds have to be severed? Pain and loss? Yes, those are real. And the deeper the love, the deeper the loss.

Many, many people don't allow themselves to love or be loved so that they can't get hurt. I don't want to live that way. I'd rather love deeply, then hurt like hell when it ends. The love is bigger than the pain—much bigger.

After all, in the final analysis performing music is an individual activity. We can't play the notes for our students . . .

I agree, in part, that music is an individual activity—because it comes from inside ourselves, and we play the notes, and the emotions are ours. But on the other hand, music is one of the most intimate ways to connect with others. It is rarely done in isolation, except when we practice or when we sit on a beach and play to the ocean waves. The learning or teaching of music is not an individual activity. It's a team effort between teacher and student. The performing of music is not an individual activity. It's a shared experience between performer and audience. Playing in an ensemble or orchestra is not an individual activity. It's a bonding of people to make something greater than their individual playing.

Certainly, I am not suggesting that the atmosphere in the studio should not be congenial and supportive, but I think we must always bear in mind that no student will study with us forever, and they are eventually going to have to stand on their own. We must always keep this as a goal of our teaching.

I know that, because your posts are always kind and congenial. And I also believe, as you do, that a goal of teaching is independence for the student. However, I think that deep attachment and support and love between student and teacher, when it's there, is the *best* way to help a student become independent. Young people who've been strongly supported and affirmed and loved for who they are, are much more likely, in my experience, to stand on their own with confidence and capability, than those who haven't had that kind of deep and unshakable relationship with at least one other significant person.

Helen

Re: Recital Question
Date: Jan. 21, 1997
Cindy Mallardo posted:

I am an adult beginner. But my teacher wants us all to do a recital in several months. Any of you know something REALLY easy that will sound more complicated than it is? I want something that will not terrify.

Cindy, first of all, congratulations on your commitment to play a recital! I have a lot of adult beginners like you who play their first recital soon after starting lessons. I think it's great. I'd be glad to send you a few suggestions.

I'd like to mention something to you about your wish to play a piece that sounds more complicated than it is. I certainly understand your wish. However, you might want to think about focusing more on the beauty of the music that you choose, or the meaning it has to you, rather than on its complexity. After all, I would hope that your recital will be about sharing your love for music, and using the gifts and skills you've developed so far to give a gift to yourself and your audience. I hope that your recital is not about showing off, or being better than the next guy, or getting your teacher's approval.

It's very human to feel these things, but I try to change my focus to higher ideals when I perform, and I encourage my students to do the same. Some of the most effective and beautiful pieces my adult students and I have played, have been the most simple. The spirit and beauty and expression in music is what gets to people's hearts.

I hope to hear back from you!

Helen

Re: What They Remember
Date: Oct. 31, 2007
John Rayworth posted:

When I ceased to be his pupil, my flute teacher's parting comment was that there was little else he could teach me. Looking at it from the other side, I've had many students who stayed with me until leaving school, and in some cases they ceased to play and it's unlikely that all of them will remember my name. However, I've also taught some really outstanding young students and was quick to pass them over to more appropriate teachers, saying "there is little else I can teach you." The strange thing is, these pupils and their families do remember me and continue to associate with me, musically and socially, and I know that I have done more for them than for many others who passed my way.

John, your comment has made me reflect on the other side, too, in this early morning before sunrise. This is interesting to think about, especially now as my studio for children is drawing to a close—now I only teach adults and do performance anxiety coaching. I've been the first teacher for most, but not all, my students.

I just realized that I don't care at all whether they remember my name. I hope, though—very much—that they remember, even in some nebulous, indefinable way, the love I poured into them. I hope they remember the attention and respect with which I treated them. I hope they still have with them, in some form, a love, joy, and interest in music that they were exposed to, or developed, through me. For some, I hope they've kept with them some life lessons that arose out of their study of music, lessons they can still use today.

If they carry even one of these things in their *hearts*, I am joyous. My name in their *minds* is of very little importance in terms of how I have seen my mission as a flute teacher these 18 years.

The vast majority of my former students have gone off, never to be heard from again. I wouldn't like it one bit if one of them spoke badly of me in public. But I have a few former students who speak my name often, with so much kindness, love, respect, and loyalty that I frequently weep with joy.

I learned a long time ago to cherish the precious love all around me, and not yearn for love that isn't mine to have.

Helen

Hugs, Jimmy

Every flutist in the world knows Sir James Galway as a performer, teacher, and conductor. Thanks to the Internet, I was lucky enough to get to know him as a person—someone who remembers his friends' birthdays, who is loving toward children, who enjoys art, reading, and gardening. That surprising email I found back in 1995 began a lovely correspondence that continues to this day.

Re: Galway Plays Liebermann
Date: Nov. 21, 1995
    Hi Helen,
    Did you hear the Liebermann? I was looking forward to seeing you.
Jimmy

Re: Your Email
Date: Nov. 23, 1995
    Dear Jimmy,
    Glad to hear from you! Yes, of course I was at your concert, I wouldn't have missed it for anything!! I enjoyed the concert a lot. Freddy was extremely tired that night, so we decided not to go backstage afterwards. I would've enjoyed saying hello to you, but instead I have a great idea. Why don't you come to my concert in January, and then *you* can come backstage to see *me!!*
Helen

Re: Thanksgiving in Hanover.
Date: Nov. 26, 1995
    Dear Jimmy,
    Thanks for your email. I have a lesson scheduled with Brooks tomorrow, so I will certainly give him your regards.
    Your playing of *Danny Boy* continues to be one of the most beautiful,

divine, stunning examples of gorgeous flute playing. How do you keep it so fresh and alive after playing it so often?

I have a 13 year old student who was in the audience. I've rarely seen a young person so in love with classical music. After he heard you play the *Badinerie*, he came to his next lesson and asked if he could play it for our student recital (which is coming up in December). It really is too hard for him, but I said yes anyway. He's been working very hard, but he's come a long way and will be able to do it, although way under tempo of course. (And I don't mean under *your* tempo, I mean under normal tempo!) You really inspired this young man to challenge himself to new limits.

What pieces are you playing on your German tour? How is Jeannie? Will you get to go home for Christmas?

Helen

Re: Your Concert and a Story
Date: Jan. 8, 1996
Dear Helen,

I suppose by now your concert is over and I am hoping it was a raging success. You deserve it. I think it was a very original thing you did and the rep choice was great.

I was ill over the New Year and had to play a concert in Cologne, live on TV, under medication. I was so out of it I left my flutes in a taxi and I did not realize it for four hours! I had a receipt from the taxi driver and called him. He still had my flutes and he delivered them to the house where I was staying. I NEVER do anything like that.

Love, *Jimmy*

Re: Musical Manicure
Date: Feb. 16, 1996
Dear Jimmy,

Two days ago, on Valentine's Day, I treated myself to something I rarely do—a manicure. When I sat down at the table, I realized that they were piping a CD into the room—your CD—and although I don't own this one, I'm very familiar with it: the *Greatest Hits #2* album.

It was such a pleasurable experience to listen to your gorgeous playing, and it felt especially nice because I've come to think of you as a friend, someone I know as a person, not just as a celebrity, and that makes the experience of listening to a CD different for me.

After awhile, I asked the manicurist, "Do you know who James Galway is?"

She stared at me blankly and shook her head. "Who's that?" she asked.

So I said, "He's a world famous flutist; he's the one playing on this CD we're hearing." She just shrugged her shoulders.

Oh, well! Some people just ain't got no culture! Many blessings to you and Jeannie on this day.

Love, Helen

Re: Report on Birthday Recital
Date: Dec. 9, 1996

Dear Jimmy,

I hope you had a great birthday. You must be in Ireland now. Good luck with your recording—it sounds like a great album and I'll be looking for it in the stores to add to my collection.

The recital went well. Your letter to my students was a hit! Everyone was so surprised and pleased. There was a lot of oohing and aahing when I read it, and I gave everyone their own copy along with their certificate at the end. The original will be posted on my bulletin board at my new studio as soon as I get there today. That way, those who didn't participate in the recital will see it as well!

Everyone played well—no major disasters. I love listening to my students play at recital. I'm so proud of them—from the littlest ones playing "Jingle Bells" to the most advanced.

Thank you for making our recital an especially exciting one. It was a privilege for all of us to play in your honor.

Love, Helen

Re: Hello!
Date: Apr. 4, 1997

Hi Helen,

How sweet of you to take the time to write to me. Of all people I think you are more busy than me. I am in the U.S. and was in Boston the night the storm hit!—33 inches recorded on Boston Common, which was straight over the road from our hotel. The concert on Tuesday evening was canceled and we played it on Wednesday. The program was the Quantz G Major with me conducting, and the "Pied Piper Fantasy" with John Williams conducting. It went very well and we had a great time in

Boston. Jeanne's cousin lives there and the family all came up for Easter. I even went to a Catholic Church and thought it was very good.

Legends is one of my favorite crossover records. Let me ask you a question. Which flute do you think I used for this one? BMG have a number of tapes I have recorded. I think the next issue will be all the Mozart concerti with Sir Neville Marriner. I also recorded the complete music for flute by Sir Malcolm Arnold, and I think that is a really good one, too. Wait till you hear it.

I wish this tour was coming down your way but I don't think it comes even near. Are you going to be around the country between now and the second week of May? I am finishing this all off in Cincinnati then coming to NY for a couple of days with Jeanne.

Best wishes for a speedy recovery. Love and a big hug.

Jimmy

Re: FLUTE List Dinner at NFA!!!
Date: May 30, 1996
Hi Helen,

Love to have dinner. Larry is going to be there too, and I'm hoping to sit at the same table as you and him. How's things? I have my last concert tonight before a three week break. Can't wait.

Love. Best wishes,

Over and OINK, *Jimmy*

Re: OINK
Date: Dec. 19, 1996
Hi, Jimmy,

Thanks for the cute Christmas email, Jimmy! Now, I have to ask you about this OINK business. Is this a shortcut for something, like ROFL means "rolling on the floor laughing," or is this a man who makes some of the most beautiful sounds on earth with his flute, trying to sound like a piglet?? Please illuminate—I'm intrigued.

Love, *Helen.*

Re: Greetings
Date: Jan. 1, 1997
Hi, Helen,

You have it the first time. This is a little greeting from one little piggy to the other. We used to write it on the opera house walls in the dressing rooms when we went on tour, and it became a secret sign among some British musicians in the early sixties. I have a friend, lawyer David Overton, and we used to write things in shorthand to each other. I suddenly signed OINK, out of the blue, and two weeks later he asked me what it was. I ROFL at the thought of my friend Dave trying to figure all this out.

Happy new year to you and the family.

Love, *Jimmy*

Re: HAPPY BIRTHDAY!!!!!
Date: Dec. 8, 1997

Hi Helen,

Thanks for remembering my birthday. I have been working really hard. I played in a concert last Saturday with Jeanne, and I conducted it as well. The Royal Choral Society performed, with more than 100 singers, and it was just delightful. I am recording the piccolo and flute concerti of Liebermann tomorrow with him conducting and the London Mozart Players playing.

I hope we will meet up before I come to Chapel Hill, so if you are over this way call me and I will put the tea pot on.

Best wishes for Christmas and the New Year,

Jimmy

Performers and Performing

Performers share their musical gifts at many different levels. The great stars share a driving passion for excellence and develop their art to its highest levels. Amateurs choose a different path, combining music with other aspects of their lives. No matter how different the level of performance, we are all the same—kindred spirits who share the love, joy and struggle of making music. In these stories, performers reveal their musical journeys and the wisdom they have discovered along the way.

To Be Good Enough or Not to Be:
That is the Question

*P*icture these scenarios:

Little Helen plays *Ave Maria* on her flute with all the passion she can muster, getting the notes and even the rhythm right, and her father says, "Can't you play with more feeling?"

Teenage Helen comes home, proudly showing her music final exam with a 98 percent on it, the highest grade in her class, and her father asks, "Where are the other two points?"

Grownup Helen gets a paid chair in a semi-professional regional orchestra, and after a concert, her mother comments, "The New York Philharmonic, it's not."

Playing the flute was the best, most special thing I did growing up, but the messages I received from my family made me feel inadequate. Now, I'm in my early 40s; I've done a great deal of deep inner work, and I have embraced a new philosophy. I finally feel good about my flute playing most of the time.

The seeds of this transformation were planted when, about eight years ago, I began my spiritual journey and realized that playing music, for me, was both an expression of my spirit and a gift to me from a source greater than myself. When I understand and acknowledge where the music really comes from, it follows directly that it is perfect just the way it is. And not only is it perfect, it has a profound purpose. In a world where there is so much pain and suffering, I believe that music—*all* music—is a vehicle of light and beauty that dispels the darkness. Each sound produced with love on a musical instrument lends healing to a wounded planet.

I now play in a supportive atmosphere. My husband likes to hear the sounds of my flute floating through our house. Once, when I had been practicing some particularly repetitive and difficult exercises, he said, "Thank you for playing your flute for me." I hadn't been playing (in my own mind) for him. He receives even my boring scales and double-tonguing exercises as a gift.

I perform in my church, where everyone adores my flute playing. They compliment me whenever and whatever I play, and when I don't play, they ask me where my flute is. My self-esteem has improved through this experience because I have something special to offer. I play with a pianist who is supportive, who never criticizes me when I make a mistake, and who always points out how well I sound on a particular passage or piece.

I have forgiven my parents for the unintentional damage they inflicted on me. In their own way, they were proud of me and did the best they could do at the time to support my musical growth. They instilled in me an appreciation of music and found a way to finance many years of flute lessons. Today I am grateful to them, while no longer buying into the old messages that don't nurture joy and self-confidence.

I started taking lessons again about two years ago, studying with a true master, someone who is internationally recognized as a flute soloist. I believe I am his least advanced student by far, but I remind myself that I am good enough just the way I am. I am not striving to sound like Jean-Pierre Rampal; my goal is to sound like Helen.

I teach my own adult flute students as well. I see them struggle with perfectionism. I listen to them criticize themselves harshly, and I see so clearly how unnecessary that is. As I try to help them see the beauty and the "good-enoughness" of their own playing, I learn to accept and even to love my own imperfect sounds. Stephanie Judy, in her wonderful book *Making Music for the Joy of It*, says that it is not our job, as amateurs, to play music perfectly, but to love it deeply. I have taken that philosophy to heart. I have come so far on this journey that I now actually enjoy my occasional solo performances, even if one or two notes are out of tune or I miss a beat. My music is good enough. I am good enough.

Music for the Love of It, June 1992
Reprinted in *Fluit*, the journal of the Dutch Flute
Society, April 2000

My First Concert

After many years pursuing my careers in teaching and grief counseling, I re-
turned to playing flute in 1990. Six years later, I was ready to give the first big
solo recital of my life. It was such a joyous event for me that I wanted to share it
with all of my flute friends. I announced my plans on FLUTE-M, the predecessor
of the FLUTE List, and responses came pouring in. As it turned out, I was very
lucky to have their advice and good wishes. The story unfolds in our FLUTE-M
correspondence, which I've kept as a loving reminder of their support.

Date: Tues., Jan. 2, 1996
From: JAMES GALWAY
To: HELEN SPIELMAN

Re: Recital Support Solicited!

Dear Helen,

What a nice letter you wrote to the FLUTE-M. You certainly put in
a lot of hours. What are you going to play in your recital? What shoes
are you going to wear? The reason for asking this is that a lot of women
practice in sneakers or just socks and then put on their best shoes for the
concert. The best shoes usually have some sort of heel and it puts the
body in a different position for playing. You may not think this matters
if you just try them on for five minutes, but try them for two hours. Are
you playing the whole recital through every day without stopping? Just
to build up the stamina, so when it comes to the Big Day, you will take it
in your stride.

I hope you are well and Jeanne* joins me in sending you both our best
wishes for the New Year.

Jimmy and Jeanne.

*Lady Jeanne Galway, Sir James' wife.

Date: Thurs., Jan. 4, 1996
From: HELEN SPIELMAN

Re: Helen's Concert Program

I've had a *lot* of FLUTE-M people ask me to tell the program for my concert, so here it is. The pieces are not that difficult, but my goal isn't to show how great a flutist I am or to get an A+ grade or win an orchestra seat. I'm aware that there are several aspects that are unconventional, but this is what I want to do, so I'm doing it!

The name of the concert is "A Circle of Listening: A Concert in a Variety of Musical Styles."

Franck Sonata in A Major (last movement)
Meditation from *Thais* by Massenet
Chaminade Concertino (Intermission follows)
Beautiful Thoughts (a lovely piece of new age piano music by David
    M. Combs that we've arranged for flute, piano and keyboards)
"Sentimentale" from the *Claude Bolling Suite* (with drums and string
    bass!)
Medley of songs from *Phantom of the Opera* (a friend's arrangement
    for piano and two keyboards—20 minutes long and sounds
    incredible!)
Encore: "The Wind Beneath My Wings"* (to add another style-
    Top 40—with piano, drums and keyboards)

When we rehearsed "Wind" for the first time, tears came to my eyes, because I never believed in my whole life that I would be playing this way—I mean, it sounded so big with the drums and all the sound and energy. I'm just feeling overwhelmed with the joy and excitement and satisfaction, and the wonderful musicians I'm getting to play with.

Helen

Date: Thurs., Jan. 4, 1996
From: HELEN SPIELMAN

Re: Helen's Concert Speech

OK, this is what I plan to say at my concert. I want to talk from my heart. Oh, god, I'm feeling more nervous about writing this to you than I think I'll be on Saturday night!

---

*"The Wind Beneath My Wings" from the movie *Beaches* (music and lyrics by Larry Henley and Jeff Silbar).

I chose music from a wide variety of styles to represent "A Circle of Listening." No matter what kind of music we listen to, music is a perfect vehicle for us to know our oneness—to get inside ourselves deep enough to feel, under all our differences of age, religion, background, even the values we hold, that place where we're all the same, where we are all deeply connected, and where our essence is purely and simply love.

From that place, it doesn't much matter that I'm up here playing and you're the audience. We're all here tonight being a circle of listening—of listening to our glorious inner selves through the music.

I'm going to read something about this from one of my favorite books, *The Listening Book* by W. A. Mathieu:

"The sounds in your life are part of a circle of listening; a tiny arc on a great circumference. When you begin a note, it comes from somewhere and keeps going forever after you have finished. It comes from your impulse to sing, from your mind and heart, all the way back to the beginning of time. It goes into thin air, into walls, patient trees, open sky, and on into vibrations there aren't names for. Part of it does, anyway. The best of it goes into the hearts and minds of others. Nothing is lost. Everything keeps going around.

"Next time you hear music (maybe your own), tune in on the intention of the musician. What does this musician really want? To make you dance? To get paid? To fill you with nostalgia? Longing? Light? Love? To praise God? To terrify you? To get famous? The answer is audible to anyone listening.

"Your intention is part of your music and never leaves it. It came from somewhere and goes somewhere. It is connected directly to the listeners and indirectly to everyone else." *Everyone else.* "When the song is over, your intention keeps going.

"Your music makes the little house where you live light up among the others. When that light shines back on you in a recognizable form ('I loved your concert.') it has not gone far enough. Be patient. When it no longer has anyone's name on it, you know that it has made its way safely into the nether regions of the Great Circle."

And then I'll follow this with the "Meditation" from *Thais*—a peaceful, quiet, reflective piece.

Helen

Date: Mon., Jan. 8, 1996
From: HELEN SPIELMAN

Re: Helen's Concert Report

Dear FLUTE-M Friends,
Well, here's what happened about my concert.

On Friday, we rehearsed with the grand piano at the church. The music went *so* well, I felt solid and confident and totally ready and so, so excited. We have a trashy piano at our church, and I had spent weeks and weeks on the phone, trying to get a local piano store to lend us a grand. Our church doesn't have enough money to rent one. After dozens of calls, I finally succeeded, and here was this absolutely magnificent six-foot Yamaha top-of-the-line grand, truly grand piano that sounded heavenly. One of the reasons for my concert was that it was a benefit concert for our grand piano fund so that one day we could have one of our own for the church.

Well, by Friday evening I heard more about the impending snowstorm, and by Saturday morning, we realized that it was serious enough to keep a lot people from coming. We were expecting a standing-room-only crowd. My friends were telling me that as they went around town and saw people they knew, that everyone was saying, "Are you going to Helen's concert?" "See you at Helen's concert." However . . .

It doesn't snow much around here in central North Carolina, so there aren't many snowplows, and when it snows even a little, everything comes to a standstill and people get totally paralyzed. A couple of people who had been out called me and said the roads were nearly impassable, that there were lots and lots of cars on the sides of the road. We haven't had snow like this in seven years.

I spent the entire Saturday sobbing. By late afternoon, the snow and ice were so bad that I had to seriously think about canceling, but I didn't want to, of course. I couldn't reach my pianist or the keyboard/drum couple, so I had no choice but to put on my concert dress and go to the church. It normally is a five-minute drive to my church. It took my husband and me 45 minutes to get there.

When we got there, David Heid (piano) and Victor and Terry Denny (drums and keyboards) were there. They had each come from two different parts of Raleigh, parts of the city that are usually about 45 minutes from here. It took them two and a half hours to get here. But here they were, saying, "Helen, if you want us to play this concert, we will." I was so touched and overcome by their loyalty and their willingness to risk driving here. We talked it over. Victor and Terry could stay in Chapel

Hill overnight, but David had to get back to Raleigh. He was worried that in two more hours the roads would be even worse. A few friends, including my wonderful teacher, had called and told me that if we decided to play the concert, they would come no matter what. I decided that no concert was worth risking people's lives, that David's safety and well-being was more important than the concert, and that it would be less painful not to do the concert at all rather than do it with our hearts not in it. So we canceled.

David left right away and got home to Raleigh safely. The rest of us waited till 8:05. Six people showed up, including one of my little 10-year-old boy students. Steve Colladay, my minister, played for about three minutes on the piano. It sounded so beautiful, the sound filled up the room (high ceiling, great acoustics) and was so smooth and gorgeous. I cried and cried.

David and Victor insisted that we reschedule for another time. I told them that I couldn't think about it then, but that if we *did* reschedule, I wasn't doing it until there were flowers in the ground. They laughed.

I was devastated. I couldn't even write to you about it yesterday. Today (Monday), I've improved some—now I'm merely depressed. I don't know if I can get up for it again. It was so much work to put this all together. It cost me so much money (well over $1,000). The disappointment is so great. I just don't know. Everyone is telling me that I shouldn't even try to make this decision till I feel better, and they're right.

They canceled church services for Sunday morning, and the piano will be taken away tomorrow, and so no one in the church ever got to see it or hear it. I don't know if the store will lend us the piano again, and I don't know how I could play this concert with the other piano after hearing this one. The other one is really terrible.

I want to tell you about your role in all this. I received so many emails from all of you. The support and love and confidence were overwhelming. I printed out every last email, and it was a thick stack of paper. I read them to myself on Saturday morning, and I put them in my flute bag, intending to read them again during my pre-concert meditation time. You folks literally came to the concert with me. I even received two phone calls from FLUTE-M people, one from a person I've never even met. I hope you don't underestimate how much you, as a group, were in my mind and heart through all this.

I thought that after this, I'd want to put my flute away for a few days and just take a break. But yesterday, I found myself wanting to play. I didn't do any serious practicing, but I was so pleased to see the desire to play arise in me. I didn't make myself play, I wanted to.

I believe there's a reason for everything, and I also believe there's a lesson for us in all our life's experiences. But what this was all about, I just don't understand. Maybe one day it will be clear to me, but right now, I'm just sad.

Thank you all for your support and love. I don't like to have to put such a "down" post on the list, but after all your involvement, I felt you deserved to hear what happened. You all are good friends.

Love, *Helen*

Date: Tues., Jan. 9, 1996
From: JAMES GALWAY
To: HELEN SPIELMAN

Re: Condolences

Dear Helen,
I heard from Brooks all about the concert, but your letter brought tears to my eyes. Fate certainly dealt you a terrible blow. I hope you will be able to do it again. I presume they have not taken the piano back as of yet? You might try rescheduling ASAP and ask the local radio station to help you out.

Love, *Jimmy.*

Date: Tues., Jan. 23, 1996
From: HELEN SPIELMAN

Re: Helen's Concert: The Sequel

Dear Flute-M Friends,
Just want to tell you that my concert is rescheduled! It will be on May 11. Everyone involved in the concert (musicians, recording person, lighting person, etc.) is able to make it on that date. My flute teacher said, "Oh, that's a good time to have your concert. All you'll have to worry about that time of year is floods." Thank you very much.

I cannot thank all of you enough for your support during this whole thing. After the concert got canceled because of the snowstorm, I received dozens of emails from all of you, sending love and comfort. These gifts of the heart came in many different ways. Some of you shared stories of similar experiences and made me feel not so alone. Some of you made a joke to make me laugh. Some of you simply said "I'm sorry." Some of you sent encouragement to go on and do it again, and you gave me strength when I felt like giving up. One person, who lives in a different country, offered me the use of his grand piano "if I lived anywhere near you." One person offered an idea to sell the tape on FLUTE-M so that you all could help the grand piano fund at my church. One provided the perfect words to describe what happened: "colossal bummer."

I received support from my "regular" friends, but *you* are the ones who do what I do: play the flute. You know what it means to prepare for a concert, musically, psychologically, physically, and spiritually. You understood what I was going through, knew what I needed, and open-heartedly sent it to me. I have printed out and kept every one of your emails, and they will always be a precious reminder for me. My gratitude is boundless.

Helen

Date: Tues., May 7, 1996
From: HELEN SPIELMAN

Re: Helen's Concert — Posting #3,578

Well, if you're as tired of reading about my concert as I am of talking about it, hit your delete key! But I did want to tell you that my solo recital is this coming Saturday.

So, here we go again. Rehearsals have been going great — I feel confident musically. I've had a hard time getting excited about the whole thing. At times I'm excited, but I'm not nearly as consumed with it as I was in January. That's probably good.

Your support of me in January was overwhelming. I'll be sure to tell you all about the concert afterwards.

With love and gratitude, *Helen*

Date: Wed., May 8, 1996
From: HELEN SPIELMAN
To: LARRY KRANTZ

Re: Helen's Concert — Posting #3,578

Larry Krantz wrote:
You are equally important to us and I wish you the best of luck for your first ever solo recital. As one who has been pulling for you since your first announcement of the recital, I must say that I am extremely excited and pleased to know that your debut is on the horizon. Your confidence and obvious love of music and the flute will surely blossom on the stage. Have a great time, play like an angel — and have you called the weather man?

Yes, Larry, I've called the weather man, several times actually. He assures me that no snow is predicted for this coming weekend in the southern United States. He's not giving me any guarantees, however, about hurricanes, tornadoes, or floods.

Helen

PS And thanks to one of our British list members who very thoughtfully informed me that it snowed in Great Britain just last week. That was very comforting.

Date: Mon., May 13, 1996
From: HELEN SPIELMAN

Re: Helen's Concert Report—Posting #357,829

I wanted a day to pass before writing to you about my concert, to let things settle in my mind. My concert was wonderful, on a lot of different levels. I want to share many things with you, because you've been with me through it all the way.

The church was packed. I think a few people even had to stand. I experienced butterflies most of the day, not terrible ones, but certainly some flutterings. I had a very well-planned day, though, which I knew from past experiences would help. I exercised, had a nap—things that kept me busy but didn't require too much focus.

After all the discussion on FLUTE-M about nerves, I was trying to observe myself and analyze exactly what I was nervous about. And I discovered that it really wasn't about playing my music well! I *knew* that I knew my music and had no fear that I would have any major disasters. I fully expected to hit a few wrong notes, which I did (not too many, just a few, I think). And not holding myself to perfection took the pressure off immensely. It was more a general kind of nervousness—would the whole thing come off OK? Would people respond well? Would I sound OK when I was talking? (I was more concerned about what I'd say than how I'd play!)

I was very satisfied with my playing. Aside from a couple of missed notes, which I didn't even waste one minute feeling bad about, I also was aware of inconsistency in tone. At times my tone sounded absolutely beautiful to me. At other times, it was lacking in focus and clarity. This is not news to me—it's something I've been working on with my teacher for a long time—to keep a *consistently* good tone.

I was also most pleased to see myself playing with expression and lack of inhibition in front of my teacher. I've had problems with this, and I've worked hard to be myself fully—to be the whole musician I am—even with him there listening. He had called me the afternoon of the concert to wish me well. He was wonderful.

Although there was a great deal of love and support for me in the audience, the people I felt the most powerful energy from were my students—especially my adult students. Their faces were in the audience beaming love and joy and support to me, and it helped me feel confident and wonderful. I didn't realize until a friend pointed it out the next day, but that is what I give to them, over and over. I model that kind of love and support for them, and here it was, unexpectedly coming back to me. It was a neat thing to contemplate.

We did get a standing ovation and I got lots of flowers, and we collected a lot of money for the grand piano fund for the church.

You folks on FLUTE-M have been incredible. I received close to 50 emails of encouragement, and good wishes. Thank you, thank you. I printed out every message and took them to the concert, intending to read them during that last half hour. But I found that I couldn't. So instead, I took the whole stack and held it to my chest and felt the love and support come through cyberspace into my heart. If you think I'm crazy, that's fine, but you were with me during the whole experience.

The most intriguing, surprising thing of the whole evening was this—I couldn't believe how fast it went. One minute, I'm sitting there waiting the last five minutes before going on stage, and the *very next minute*, it was intermission. Had we played through all three of our pieces? Did we finish the whole Chaminade? And the second half flew by, and then it was over. Lots of people did tell me afterwards that I, and all the musicians, looked like we were really having fun up there, which we were. And I guess, as the saying goes, time flies when you're having fun.

Would I do it again? I don't know. As far as the actual performing goes, yes, yes—I'd love to do another recital. As far as all the work involved in setting it up, making the arrangements, dealing with the hassles, and the financial expense, I don't know.

We do the whole concert again on Wednesday night in Raleigh. Maybe after that, I'll have some more thoughts. Anyway, thanks for listening— and much more than that, thanks for being my friends and for all the generous things you have done to help make my first recital a fantastic experience.

With much love,
Helen

Date: Thurs., May 16, 1996
From: HELEN SPIELMAN

Re: Helen's Concert — Posting #12,844,035,396.73A

Excuse me while I bubble over with joy for a moment. I just had my lesson with my teacher. We spent 45 minutes of the hour talking about my concert. He said that he had never heard me sound better, that he thought the whole thing as a package was excellent, that he left walking three feet above the ground because he was so proud of me.

Last night, we did the concert again in Raleigh, at David's church. It was a lot of fun, again, although the turnout was tiny — 15 people. And of course, it was raining horribly. I wouldn't dream of giving a concert on a pretty day.

Helen

Date: Sun., May 12, 1996
From: HELEN SPIELMAN

Re: A Review? For Me?

Ellen Zimmerli wrote:
Hi, I have the good fortune of living in the "Southern Part of Heaven" Chapel Hill and was able to attend Helen's recital. Let me tell you, it was lovely. Her personality certainly comes out in her playing. The weather held out. Fortunately, the high winds and flash floods circled around Chapel Hill. We only had a short storm in the afternoon. It is a good thing that they missed us, since not 20 miles away at the RDU airport the roof was blown off the American Airlines terminal and the airport was put to a halt!

I couldn't believe this when I saw it on my screen today. Thanks, Ellen, for your warm and generous remarks. I feel very flattered! And of course, no self-respecting reviewer of any concert of *mine* would fail to give a complete and detailed description of the weather.

And by the way, not only did the American Airlines roof blow off, but there were extensive power failures not five minutes away from the church. My friend called my house an hour and a half before curtain time to see if the concert was still on, because her entire neighborhood lost power. My husband answered the phone. He didn't tell me about it till after the concert. He knew I would've gone bonkers.

Helen

A Professional Amateur: Jeanne Baxtresser

I first met Jeanne Baxtresser at the National Flute Association Convention in 1997. Her passion for music has been a continuing source of inspiration and wisdom through the years, as you will see from this report of my first conversation with Jeanne.

Jeanne Baxtresser, principal flutist of the New York Philharmonic, was the guest speaker at the annual Flute Lovers' Luncheon at the National Flute Association Convention in August. At the luncheon, sponsored by the Amateur Resources Committee, we were both seated at the head table, which gave me the opportunity to chat with this charming, sincere, enthusiastic woman. She inspired such excitement in me that I began writing this as soon as I got home, before I unpacked my bags.

Jeannie told the 200 flutists in attendance that when people ask her what she does for fun, she answers that she plays the flute. Their reaction is usually, "No, I mean, what do you do when you stop working, how do you spend your leisure time?" And Jeannie answers, "I play the flute! I can imagine no more pleasure than playing music with others; that's what makes me happy and what I choose to do." She explained that she regularly plays for free at retirement communities, "for my soul." She gives the gift of music, and receives the gift of being listened to by an unconditionally appreciative audience. She encourages her students to do the same.

Although Jeannie teaches students from all over the world at the highest level (at The Juilliard School, Manhattan School of Music, Carnegie Mellon University, and privately), she also enjoys teaching amateurs. She says, "I love the experience of teaching students who simply want to enhance their ability on the flute and in music. Even if they decide not to use their music professionally, they can enjoy becoming the best flutists they can be."

She encouraged us: "Study with a teacher who shares your passion.

Don't study with anyone who doesn't love and nurture you. You should be able to practice guilt-free, in whatever amount of time you have available to you. If you practice tone exercises for five minutes, then tell yourself 'Yes, I did my tone work today,' and feel satisfied.

"The greatest learning curve," she continued, "comes at the beginning and the end of your practice session. At the beginning, you're eager and open and ready to work. At the end, you know you only have a few minutes left to accomplish your goal for that day, so you push a little harder. In the middle of your session, you can get complacent. Therefore, practice less time, but more frequently, and you'll be more efficient."

Jeannie's mother was a professional pianist, and her father was a passionate amateur. She poignantly stated that she has carried his love of listening to music with her all of her life. Her brother is an amateur violist who gets up at 5 A.M. every morning to practice for an hour before going to work with his road construction crew.

At age 21, when Jeannie was just starting her career, she was offered a position as first flutist of the Montreal Symphony. She didn't know whether to accept it because she'd had so little experience with the financial aspects of the music business. She didn't know whether the salary was appropriate, or whether she was being offered less money because she was a woman. Her mother was on a concert tour at the time, so Jeanne called for advice from a family friend, Rafael Druian, concertmaster of the Cleveland Orchestra under George Szell. He asked her, "If they invited you to play with the symphony for no money at all, would you want to do it?" Her immediate and heartfelt answer was "Of course!" Her love of playing was so powerful that it put all else in perspective. She took the job and launched her orchestral career. Nevertheless, Jeanne told us, the joy of her storybook musical life has been in the journey, not in her achievements.

For her, the person who most exemplified passion for music was Leonard Bernstein. Often after performing a piece, with the audience cheering and clapping, the members of the orchestra sat for fifty or sixty seconds, waiting for Mr. Bernstein to "come back." He had been transported to another world of human experience and had taken the entire orchestra with him on the journey.

"People respond more to encouragement than to negativity," said Jeannie. "When cueing an instrumentalist, Zubin Mehta looks like he is expecting the most beautiful solo ever heard. That brings out the best people have to give."

Halfway through her presentation, Jeannie's husband appeared at the door and she invited him in. He seemed hesitant to interrupt her talk by crossing such a large room filled with tables of eager listeners. With a twinkle in her eye, she beckoned him again, saying, "Come on, honey. There's even some pie here for you." She introduced him as David Carroll, associate principal bassoonist of the New York Philharmonic, and her best friend in the orchestra.

"I want to do more and more to bring people into music. I have an equal passion for both professionals and amateurs, not just the superstars. We might spend our days doing different things, but the meaning of music in our lives is the same for everyone.

"I think every musician should play some of the time without thought of personal advancement, with the experience of giving as the only goal. It's so natural for professionals to think 'I hope I get a good review' or 'I hope I get more concerts.' These aren't idle thoughts; they're necessary for survival. But beyond these considerations, music must be given just for the joy of it. Making music should not be for personal gain but to enrich our lives."

My life was enriched by meeting this special person who shared her thoughts and memories. Although Jeanne Baxtresser is at the highest level that a professional musician can achieve, she is a true amateur—one who loves music deeply, for all the right reasons.

Music for the Love of It, December 1997

Playing with James Galway for Flutewise

"*I* saw your picture in the paper," said Jimmy to my 12-year-old student. "Are you famous in your school now?" Jenna, not quite believing the real James Galway was talking to her, gave the most detailed, articulate answer she could muster: "No."

This small exchange characterized the overwhelming love and attention that James Galway gave us last night during his concert in Chapel Hill. He and his outstanding ensemble played a gorgeous program of Baroque music, but during intermission, he came to the front of the hall between the first row of seats and the stage, where my group of 14 children and adults were waiting, ready to play. Jimmy made an announcement about *Flutewise Magazine*, and then he and his wife, Jeannie, joined us as we played the Brian Boru "March," the "Merry Widow Waltz," "Loch Lomond," Largo from the Dvořák *New World Symphony*, a Welsh folk song, and the "Galway Piper."

Between two pieces, Jimmy played a run of notes. "Hey," I quipped, "stay with the rest of the group!"

"I got too excited," he responded.

I'd expected that the audience would be walking, talking, and doing what most audiences do during intermission. Instead, the entire hall of 1,600 people stood and listened attentively, enchanted by the most famous flute player in the world making music with children and amateur adults, looking as though he was enjoying himself immensely.

At the end of our performance, he told me that I was "the best conductor he'd played under all week." I responded, "I don't know a thing about conducting. I was just waving my hand in the air."

"No, no, Herbert von Karajan would be proud," he joked.*

The parents of the students asked incredulously, "How ever did you set this up, Helen?" I'd sent Jimmy an email, asking if he would like us to play for him as a promotion for Flutewise, the British organization to

*Herbert von Karajan conducted The Berlin Philharmonic Orchestra, 1955–1989.

encourage young flute players. Not long afterward, my phone rang and I heard his jovial Irish accented voice saying, "Let's do it." It was that simple.

I thought the rest of the planning would be simple as well, but this event required a great deal of my time and energy for several weeks, a time of whirlwind phone calls and emails, not only from Jimmy. Liz Goodwin, the head of Flutewise in England, who gave me so much support; the people at Theodore Presser who distribute the magazine in the U.S. and sent materials; Jimmy's agent, who coordinated arrangements; the local production staff who engineered all the details; the box office manager who arranged discount tickets for my students—all did their jobs outstandingly well.

I visited the hall in advance of the concert date and met with the house manager to make sure all would go smoothly. I sent out press releases to newspapers and TV stations. We made a gigantic, colorful banner that said, "James Galway and Chapel Hill Flute Students Celebrate *Flutewise Magazine*." I had to call the performing students several times—all fourteen of them. And of course, we had to rehearse our music.

We only had time for two rehearsals. I gave special thought to placing the students for a balanced sound and placed each beginner on a stand with an advanced student. I stapled the music into matching colored folders. One of the 12-year-olds noticed how neat the music looked and said, "Awesome!" Alison had laryngitis and couldn't play, but she came to rehearsal anyway to learn how to make the pieces more musical.

I noticed an interesting phenomenon in the week before the concert. Martha and Brittany, Virginia and Allison and Lauren arrived at their lesson, eager to practice their "James Galway music." We put aside their regular repertoire to concentrate on the performance, and I was impressed at how well the students, even the ones who usually struggle, played. Too bad they aren't this motivated with their scales and etudes, I thought, amused.

During the week prior to the event, stories and photos appeared about our group in three newspapers. Two of the newspapers used my press release and a phone interview with me to write their pieces. One paper sent a photographer to our second rehearsal, but she arrived just as 14 flutes had been cleaned and put back in cases. All the players were more than happy to take the flutes back out and play our pieces again while the photographer snapped away. A reporter came on a different evening, and some of my students drove back to my home yet again to participate in the interview.

My students were beside themselves with excitement. They came to the concert early to help distribute the free issues of *Flutewise Magazine* to flute-playing members of the audience. They surprised me with a big, lovely flower arrangement. None of my students have ever given me a group gift before, and as they crowded around, so unexpectedly, to present the flowers to me, I was overwhelmed with love and gratitude.

The students gave Jimmy a gift, too. Each of them made or wrote a card, and I tied them together with a big blue bow. I gave the stack to Jimmy before the concert while he was rehearsing and I was setting up music stands. He seemed genuinely pleased. Jenna made a glittery gold star on her computer, Elsa hand-painted notes on a music staff, and Rachel pasted the words "The Magic Flute" in Chinese into her card.

Jenna wrote, "I hope to someday be as good as you." The sentiment summed up the deeper aspects of what occurred last night. My children were not only inspired to love their flutes more, but they learned, I hope, that through music they can do good in the world. By promoting Flutewise, they made others aware that this organization exists, and by increasing its membership, more needy children will be given flutes to play and scholarship money to study music.

They learned something else, too, about generosity of spirit. This concert was second-to-last on James Galway's two-month-long American tour. He must have been exhausted. He could have spent intermission in his dressing room with his feet up, sipping juice or closing his eyes to relax. Instead, he gave us his attention and energy and humor. And by doing so, everyone won. James Galway got a forum to promote the organization of which he is president, and Flutewise gained more familiarity in the U.S. The audience was enthralled by the stark contrast of an international superstar playing right beside children and adults who'd just begun to learn their first notes, all having an equally good time. My students received a level of recognition that I hope inspires them to commit more deeply to music and the flute, and a magical memory to keep always.

When Jimmy came out on stage, he told the audience how happy he was to be in Chapel Hill, to see the colors of the changing autumn leaves, more beautiful than any artist could paint. He was glad to see his old friend Brooks de Wetter-Smith, the flute professor at the university, and Jimmy mentioned me, saying that I've inspired a lot of kids. I must admit that I felt gratified to hear it, but what I got from this experience went all the way down to my soul, where the joy of sharing music at its finest and the love of children at its deepest, resides.

Flutewise Magazine, December 1998

Helen's Flute Flop

I was the soloist yesterday for Easter Sunday at my church. I played with a new pianist who I knew would not be a super musician, but would be better than the one I'd refused to play with at Christmas. I really wanted to play yesterday because besides being Easter, it was also my birthday.

I collaborated with her on the choice of music, pieces with which she was familiar and weren't too difficult for her. She had the music for the past three months, she practiced diligently, and our rehearsal last week went well.

As I tell the rest of this story, please remember that I attend a very informal church, where we do all styles of music and services are casual.

Our opening piece, "What a Wonderful World,"* went fine. The meditation piece, J.S. Bach's "Jesu, Joy of Man's Desiring," she miscounted in one section. I was a bit annoyed, but we got back on track and it was OK.

Just before we began our third piece during the offertory, I thanked everyone for their lovely birthday wishes. I said that I had hoped I'd wake up that morning resurrected, with 30 fewer pounds, no grey hair, and wrinkle-free.

Everyone chuckled. I wished everyone a happy Easter, and I announced the title of our New Age piece, "Beautiful Thoughts."**

About three-fourths of the way through, she had a piano solo, and I was waiting to come back in, and I waited, and waited . . . she went off somewhere very pretty but nothing that was ever before heard by me. I kept listening for a place to come in . . . nothing. I thought, OK, I'll just jump in and start, but there was no place that was harmonically good, and I knew if I just started, I couldn't trust her to find me, as I would trust the other pianists I usually play with (who wouldn't have gone off like this in the first place). And of course, all my years of training and expe-

*"What a Wonderful World" (music and lyrics by George Weiss and Bob Thiele).
**"Beautiful Thoughts" by David M. Combs.

rience said, "Don't stop no matter what," and all my years of drumming into my students' heads shouted, "Don't stop, keep going, the pianist will find you." But I just knew it wasn't going to happen.

By now, it was clear to the audience that I was lost, and of course they were thinking that *I* messed up. And from somewhere inside of me came: "Help! I need some resurrecting here!" And the entire congregation cracked up laughing, and it gave me and the pianist enough time to say, "Top of page 6." We started there together, and finished the piece, along with long and strong applause—not for the music, I think, but support for us getting through. And I was up there laughing as I acknowledged the applause, and the minister hugged me, saying she didn't need to give a sermon that day, that I had shown what calling for help, and acting with grace and poise, were all about. And I said that that morning, my friend had sent me an Easter/birthday email and wrote: "She hath risen," and I guess I had. :) Everyone laughed again.

Later, having a birthday lunch with my husband and friends, I thought about years past, when I would have berated myself hatefully: "I'm so angry at that pianist for messing up this beautiful music. I'm so upset that everyone thinks I messed up when it wasn't really me. I need to go tell everyone that it was her fault, not mine. I ruined the service, I ruined my birthday, I'm going to feel bad all day, maybe all week. I'm a terrible flutist. I'm depressed. I hate myself. No one will really like me anymore or want to hear me play again." And on and on and on . . .

But I felt not a whiff of that yesterday. I felt great. I felt safe with these people. I've played in this church for 16 years, was music director for 11, and something like this has never happened to me there, or in any other performing situation. I thought the whole thing was hilarious! I laughed and laughed and felt wonderful! I felt that I'd acted like a true professional. I didn't care that *a mistake* had happened, because I rose above it and turned it into something wonderful, and I allowed myself to feel my *humanity*. Wow, have I ever come a long way. I may not have been resurrected, but I felt liberated.

How I wish my students had been there! I'd rather that they had witnessed this than all my so-called perfect performances. I wish my students had seen and heard all the people who complimented me on my music—those who said they loved my music with no comment on the blooper at all, who were so sincere in their praise, who just didn't care about the mistake.

And those who did comment on the mess-up, commented positively! I wish my students had been there to hear the absolute lack of even one negative word about the mistake. I wish they'd learn that when I complimented them on their recital performance, and they said, "Oh, but I messed up and played a Bb instead of a B-natural," that they are not perceiving the true nature of their performance.

Please post your story of performances you may have had in which you felt that you were able to drop some of your old self-criticizing perfectionism despite a mistake or less-than-perfect performance.

May I dare ask, especially, for some of the elite professional solo artists on the FLUTE List to answer? I recently heard two such artists (a flutist and a pianist) talk on a similar topic and it was so touching and helpful.

> Happy spring holidays to everyone!
> *Helen*

FLUTE List, April 12, 2004

Inspiration Found:
Master Class with Wissam Boustany

I n a master class last week, Wissam Boustany told a young flutist, "Make the moment sparkle with your energy. Challenge yourself to go beyond what is comfortable." Wissam follows his own advice. He is vibrant with energy and goes far beyond ordinary limits. His visit to Raleigh and Chapel Hill last week was exciting, stimulating, and immensely pleasurable.

I first met Wissam on the Internet, and when he mentioned that he would like to come to my area, I took it upon myself to connect him with RAFA, the Raleigh Area Flute Association, and with the University of North Carolina, both of which sponsored him for a master class and concert. Consequently, I had six days in a row of activities revolving around his visit. The first was a classy reception complete with scrumptious Middle Eastern food at the home of his cousin who lives 10 minutes from me. Wissam Boustany grew up in Lebanon and now lives in London, so the fact that his cousin is practically my neighbor is amazing. My first in-person impression of Wissam was that he is warm, casual, intense, genuine, and engaging, all of which turned out to be true after I got to know him better.

Most master class teachers coach the technical aspects of playing the flute, guiding students to use their embouchures or fingers in various ways, or telling them how to play a phrase differently. Wissam focuses very little on such matters. He concentrates his efforts on inspiring flutists to play with more love.

With great energy and intensity, with colorful imagery and expressive body language, he says, "The miracle of flute playing is that you take something from out there—something you can't see—and you bring it into your lungs. What comes out is light and brilliance and warmth and energy and color.

"Every note, every single note, is worthy of your care and love. Each note has a life to live: the beginning of the note, the middle, and the end.

You have choices: how do I make it shiver into life? Do I swell it, fade it, play it with vibrato? You've got to make that decision in the space of every eighth note.

"The intake of air is like a mother, giving birth to the sound. Release the air molecule by molecule. Support doesn't come from a bunch of muscles. Support comes from your soul." A student whose profession is in computers said that he was losing too much air, and Wissam responded with his typical sense of humor, "You're using too many air megabytes."

"Every phrase you play is a life coming forth. It must not be made to fit into a tick, tock, tick, tock. The metronome is the worst thing ever invented. It sucks."

Wissam repeated how important it is to take each moment and do the best with it. His goal is to bring out the music in each person in a lively way so that they can communicate that music to others. "If I take a risk," he explains, "the music flies. If I let the music play by itself, it's OK, but it's ordinary."

Wissam's playing radiates an intensity that electrifies the listener. His concerts succeed in turning an ordinary evening into one of those never-to-be-forgotten musical moments. I have rarely heard a flutist play with such passion and direct communication with the audience. Even though he made some small technical errors that would be detected only by someone familiar with the repertoire, the heartfelt expressiveness of the sounds he created transcended all thoughts of right or wrong notes and went right to the realm of the spirit.

One of Wissam's main theses is to play music by memory. He plays all his concerts that way and entreats students to do the same. While pianists and violinists often memorize their music, flutists rarely do, and Wissam's memorization is impressive. Without music in front of him, he can move his body, use his face, and be free in a way I have not seen any other flutist do.

"With the printed music in front of you, you have to follow it. Without the music, you have to look inside for the notes. If you play by heart, whatever you learn will go deeper. Don't worry about your fingers. The more you trust in the sound, the more your fingers will slide to the notes."

Over and over again, Wissam asked us to be inspired, and to play with inspiration. "The beauty in music comes from our inner desire, and from our will. The will behind the sound *is* the sound. Music doesn't come from the flute—it comes from the inner intention. Develop that fierce desire, and play so that every corner of the room is inspired."

Wissam gave a private master class for my students and encouraged us to use mistakes and failures for motivation. He emphasized that we need to praise ourselves for the good things we've accomplished and the positive gains we make each day in our practice. Instead of telling ourselves that our fingers are too slow, we should liberate ourselves by choosing words that inspire us, in the spirit of the music we are trying to play: "One more time, for joy's sake."

"Notice," said Wissam, "how a note becomes silence. Silence becomes a note. You're playing a divine note. Shine your way through into the silence."

"The act of going up a scale is symbolic of something divinely beautiful in life. Reach up beyond life; look up at the light."

Wissam shared with us his philosophy of performance. "The audience comes into the hall with their thoughts of money, responsibilities, inadequacies floating in their heads. Just when they leave those thoughts for a moment, and think, 'Hey, this is great,' will you give up? No, give more and more and MORE!!! Every concert you give is as important as 10 lessons for what you learn about yourself. Don't mistake sureness for nerves. Sureness is knowing what you want to do, and that will always shine through your jitters."

I was a little nervous about taking my private lesson with Wissam. I hadn't had a lesson with anyone other than my own teacher for two decades. I've always had a strong resistance to memorization and improvisation, and in the space of two hours, Wissam had me playing a page and a half of my solo by heart, and had me improvising for the first time in my life.

When we stopped, I cried. He thought I was upset, but I cried because music touches so deep inside me. I saw in that moment how many limitations I place on myself, and how limitless are my possibilities if I just open to them. I cried because of the beauty of what I can do that I haven't yet acknowledged. I cried because my soul was moved by this man who didn't tell me I played well or poorly, but who unconditionally accepted my music as it is without judgment, and encouraged me to break through a lifetime of resistance in one morning.

Wissam said, "The point between two notes is magic." The concert in Chapel Hill had a magical aura to it. I could feel the spark in the air and see it between Wissam and the pianist, Greg McCallum. I felt the hush of awe during Wissam's duet with my teacher, Brooks de Wetter-Smith. The enthusiasm of the standing ovation Wissam received was exhilarating—such an expression of appreciation in this town is rare.

To a college student who seemed lethargic, Wissam urged, "No matter where you're going with your music, all your brain cells and heart cells are buzzing with life." This extraordinary man is buzzing with life on many levels. He has founded Towards Humanity, an organization that uses music to bring peace and support to people in war-torn countries. At the concerts, Wissam passionately entreated the audiences to work for peace, which he calls the "burning, burning, burning need of our time."

Wissam has followed his own heart, and the path he has chosen is unique. He's a different kind of performer and teacher, and while the more standard approaches are important and valid, Wissam shares a message that people are hungry for. He gives of himself with exceptional vitality, depth, strength, and conviction. He can ask us to be inspired and to inspire others because he is the essence of inspiration himself. "Never go faster than the joy you can feel in every note," he says. Wissam feels the joy in every note, in every person, in every moment of life.

His master class was entitled, "In Search of Inspiration." This past week, I found it.

Music for the Love of It, August 1998

It's Not About the Flute:
Mark Thomas Revealed

"What am I doing here?" I ask myself as I drive down the North Carolina interstate. "Whatever will I ask him?" A brilliant question flashes through my mind, and I practice it aloud: "What is your favorite color?"

I'm on my way to interview Mark Thomas, internationally known flutist and founder of the National Flute Association. My instructions from Mary Jean Simpson, editor of *The Flutist Quarterly*, were explicit: "Find out about the inner Mark Thomas. Everyone already knows about his professional accomplishments." I didn't anticipate the twisting path that Mark and I would walk to find the hidden treasure inside him.

I meet Mark and his wife Judith at the Grandover Resort, about halfway between their home in Charlotte, North Carolina, and mine in Chapel Hill. It's a clear, sunny day in February as we make ourselves comfortable in a small, quiet coffee shop with windows overlooking peaceful greenery. I am immediately at ease with them. Mark looks distinguished, with broad shoulders, gray hair, and the self-assured groundedness that fits his 71 years. His shirt is embroidered on the pocket with his name and a flute. Judith, 58, has an engaging smile and the classic beauty that comes from inner grace and peace.

Mark takes charge and begins the interview by himself, going on for a full 10 minutes about his professional life. I interrupt his flow, reminding him that I'm here to learn about personal topics, and I ask about his interest in trains. His heather-blue eyes light up and his voice is animated.

"We have a garden railroad. We're in a club of about 75 couples, all of whom have a similar 'G' scale, which is approximately 1:24 (1 inch = 24 inches). The engines, each about a foot long, are exact replicas of a real train from the 1900–1925 era. We started this hobby two years ago as novices by digging out the backyard, positioning rocks, building a pond and waterfall, and laying 200 feet of track, with 150 feet more that we plan to add soon. The transformer that runs the train is inside the house.

The whistles and engines of the train, which you can hear from a block away, sound real. We built the houses, tunnels, and bridges. Our covered bridge has 3,000 hand-laid shingles; we thought we were going to die putting them in. Our scene is a typical mountain town that we named Fluta, Colorado, after Fruita, a real town in that state. On the second floor of one of the buildings there's a sign that says 'flute lessons,' and in another spot, 'flute repair.' People come from all over to see our display. We have so much fun, and it's a great diversion from music. Everyone thinks I'm too focused on my flute life."

A waiter stops by our table to refill our water glasses. "When I kept being told that I was too caught up in music, I became certified as a graphoanalyst. I'm a handwriting expert in a court of law. This skill helps me to teach flute students because I discern almost everything about them from their handwriting, and therefore know how to handle each student individually. An analysis takes about eight hours to do, and I took two years to become certified. At first I thought, 'This is nuts.' But then I became aware of the benefits." I smile and pretend to hide my handwriting from him.

Because I know that our inner lives are deeply influenced by our developmental years, I prompt him to tell me about his childhood.

"I came along during the Great Depression, on April 24, 1931, in Lakeland, Florida. That's the eve of St. Mark's Day, and I hope I didn't dishonor the saint too much. My father was a minister, and my mother had been a child prodigy on violin and keyboard, later holding a position on the faculty of the Detroit Conservatory of Music. She had perfect pitch. I have relative pitch, and I think it's *reasonably* relative—I've been able to hold jobs and not get fired *too* often. Then came the Depression, where everyone was hurting for food. I know what it's like to get clothes from Goodwill. All of us in that generation have worked hard, because we felt it deeply and don't ever want to go back. My mother used to give piano lessons for 50 cents. The first flute I ever had was a piece of junk that cost $35. Where my parents got that money, I'll never know. I learned how to play that flute incorrectly pretty well."

Now that he's mentioned the word *flute*, Mark can't resist telling about how he learned to play flute and who his teachers were. This time, I'm quick. "I've got to stop you here, because we're getting too professional." He says okay, but goes right back to the story!

Eventually he comes around to telling me how he met Judith. Ah ha, I think, now we're getting somewhere. "I first met her when she was 13, when she attended a flute clinic I gave. She took a few lessons from me. Later I taught a clinic at Lebanon Valley College in Pennsylvania, where

Judith was studying. She had been randomly assigned to help me get around the campus. The next thing I know, she gave up her scholarship and transferred to the American University flute program, near to me, in Washington, D.C. One thing led to another, and now it's been 38 years.

"We have two children—Elizabeth, who has her own business in Colorado, and Trevor, whose birthday is today. From a very early marriage I have three boys: Jeff, who is a flute maker, and Scott and David, who live in Dallas. They're all good people."

That's about all Mark can stand. His conversation goes back to flutes, flute design, flute studies. I patiently ask, "Tell me what you were like as a teenager. Did you get in trouble a lot or were you studious?"

"Because of the Depression, I felt a lot of fear. We never knew where the next dime for food would come from. My parents went their separate ways, and in the 10th grade I was sent to live with my brother in Minnesota. I spent a couple years out there and then went East. I guess I was very insecure, and by the time I thought girls were nicer than boys, I was afraid to ask anybody out."

Before he can jump back to something professional, I ask, "In the context of the Depression era and your fear, was your family loving and supportive, or was there tension or some level of unhappiness?"

"Yes, there was economic stress that created tension, and then I went off to my brother's and had separation anxiety, having left all my friends and adjusting to a very different life in Minnesota. I had a hard time making the change, but all of it made me stronger, and hey, I got lucky."

He points to Judith, which prompts me to ask her, "Tell me what Mark was like when you first met him, his personal qualities. What did you see in him that interested you? And then tell me which of those things have stayed with him and which have changed over the years you've been together?"

Judith's voice and face soften as she reminisces. "When I first met him, he was entertaining, animated, kind, and had a boundless enthusiasm for flute and teaching. Those qualities haven't changed. He's a very thoughtful, sweet husband. He always remembers anniversaries and birthdays. Once he gets interested in something, he throws himself into it, like the railroad, and like our dog whom we just lost. He and Indi were inseparable. We're going to pick up another German shepherd in three weeks."

I glance over at Mark. His elbow is on the armrest, his chin resting in his palm, his eyes, filled with grief, sorrow, and pain, staring unseeingly out the window. My heart goes out to him at the loss of his beloved pet.

In a flash of an instant, I realize that Judith could be an ally to help me probe deeper into Mark's essence. "Thanks for sharing all those complimentary things with me. It's great to see a long marriage in which the couple still loves and respects each other. But, as you know, there's hardly a husband alive who doesn't have some aggravating trait or habit. What peeves you the most about Mark?"

"He's very persnickety and exacting about things. Sometimes it seems silly to me that everything has to be in a perfect spot. That's the most annoying thing."

"I can relate to that," I said. "I have a husband just like him. In your opinion, what has been Mark's deepest sorrow in life?"

"Wow." Long pause. "I'd have to say that it would be his loss of childhood when his parents split up and he didn't remain living with either one of them. He was born to a Welsh father and an American mother, and they'd never had a typical family; they didn't eat supper together, and lived more separately than most. And to not be told, at age 14 or 15, the reason he couldn't stay with his family in Florida, instead being sent out West. His parents hadn't gotten along or spoken to each other for years, but at least the family was intact until that point. But you'll have to ask him."

Mark jumps in. "Yes, that's it. That's why I can relate to students' problems, because I've been there and done that."

I comment, "Most young persons are deeply affected by the modeling they see in their parents. You've come from a family that split up and was not in a good state. Yet you've established a uniquely special marriage. I'm wondering—how were you able to do that, rather than repeating what you had seen in your childhood?"

"Well, Judith certainly provided a stabilization. I never met my grandparents. My brother and sister did well for themselves, but I was the baby, and we were seven years apart. We were three separate children. I was the last one standing when everything fell apart. I do think my early upbringing has given me a great deal of compassion."

"Mark, tell me, what is the thing you're most proud of in your lifetime, that does not have to do with the flute or music?"

"Getting Judith to say 'yes.' Being a decent father." Again his eyes fill with tears.

"Those are good things to feel proud of," I say softly. "Can you tell me what your tears are about?"

"Maybe childhood lost."

"I'm so sorry."

Judith adds, "He's proud that our children want to keep up with him as closely as they do."

We stop for a moment to take photos.

Then Mark exclaims, "Boy, you have some tough questions! You're a good interviewer. When I read your last article in the Raleigh Area Flute Association newsletter, I thought, 'So this is who is going to rake us over the coals.'"

"Hey!" I respond gleefully.

Judith adds, "The thing I find interesting is you're not letting him keep up his facade. Because he's very good at that."

Mark responds, "Well, there's a professional you and then there's the real you."

And Judith replies, "Very few people know the real Mark."

"Can you tell me more about the fact that few people know the real Mark?"

"He's always been busy being the showman, so the public perception of him is different from what his family sees. He likes to joke and enjoy the relaxed moments, to sit back with a bowl of popcorn watching movies, to putter around the house. Given the choice, he would spend more time doing these things if he didn't feel so responsible for the other activities in his life."

"What is the reason you think he keeps his facade up? Of course, everyone does that some, but usually there's a reason behind it, such as shyness, insecurity, introversion, sorrow, shame, or pain. What is his facade about?"

Judith continues, "I think there may be some carryover from feeling insecure in childhood, wondering whether people really like or love you. If you don't let anyone know where your goat's tied, no one can get it. The other side is that he's the ultimate salesman. He sold himself to me! Our son says, 'If I could just learn to work a room the way Dad does, I could sell ice cubes to Eskimos.' If I take him to one of my professional functions (I'm a nurse in a chronic pain center, working for anesthesiologists), he'll ask me at the door, who do you want to meet? And he will proceed to work the room, meeting people and making contacts, and it's not even his function."

"How interesting," I say to Mark. "My husband is an anesthesiologist. Would you like to go to one of our functions and help me out that way?"

"With your line of questions," Mark shoots back, "you won't have any trouble working a room." The three of us break into laughter.

I start to ask Mark my next question. He holds the mike in position, but pretends to shake and quake with fear at what my next question might be. More laughter from our corner of the room.

"What do you do for physical fitness? Do you do sports?"

"I have a treadmill that I sometimes use at 5:45 A.M. and a shovel for my railroad, and I play tennis. In high school I played track. I ran the 440."

"In general, do you enjoy good health?"

"Yes, I'm healthy. Eight years ago, I had an annual physical, and despite the doctor's hesitation, Judith insisted that I get a PSA test. The test showed a malignant tumor in the prostate and I had surgery, and now my tests are normal. Recently, I asked the doctor how long I would have lived had not Judith insisted on the PSA. He said about two years. So I owe her my life." Mark's eyes fill with tears again, and he has to stop talking to calm his breathing and dab at his eyes. "I keep a pretty active life; nothing slows me down, though I'm gradually starting to cut back."

"What is the one most important thing that you still want to accomplish in your life that does not have to do with the flute or music?"

Long pause, and I wait through dead silence for his answer. "That's a very difficult question."

Judith says, "She's making you think. This is a good thing."

More silence. "Not the flute, and not music," he repeats, as though questioning, what else is there in life?

Finally, "Well, if I got away from music more, it would be spending time with the kids and grandchildren. I have five grandchildren, and three great-grandchildren."

I address Mark. "Both of you strike me as being incredibly young for your age in your looks, attitude, activity level, and your interest in everything. But as you get older, what do you think will be your biggest fear?"

Again, Mark begins to cry, and in a fragile, shaky voice, answers, "Dying alone."

I empathize. "Yes, I think it's part of the human condition; we have to live with that fear. Do you have religious beliefs?"

Mark says, "Yes, we're Episcopalians, the religion in which I grew up. I work at the church as a verger."

Judith touches his knee and admonishes gently, "Listen to her question, dear. She asked about your religious beliefs."

I try to guide Mark a bit. "Do you have a regular spiritual practice? For instance, do you go to church, pray by yourself, get out in nature?"

"All of the above."

"Do you find that when fears or sorrows come up in your life, you turn to your beliefs for help at that time?"

"Yes."

"Is that helpful?"

"It calms." Mark seems to have a hard time speaking now, because of the emotion welling up in him. "Especially in times of stress. And sometimes it directs when I don't know what to do in a situation. Sometimes direction means to do nothing. I believe that if it's supposed to be, it will be, and if you're not supposed to do that, there's a reason why that door got shut. Because that other one is supposed to open, but you didn't know it, and it might be even better." He takes a big breath, then revives enough to ask, "Where did you learn to come up with all these questions?"

I truthfully inform him that I'm winging it, that this is my first interview.

"It is?" he asks incredulously. "This is the toughest interview I've ever been in. I love it! I've been interviewed in magazines, newspapers, on radio, TV, but never one like this! This is tough."

I ask, "Is that OK with you?"

"Sure!"

Judith adds, "It's because she's not letting you be just your public person."

I'm aware of the special energy flowing between the three of us now. "I'm loving this interview. I'm so glad Mary Jean asked me to do it— otherwise I would never have met either of you, and I think you're fabulous people."

Mark corrects me, "No, we're just people who happen to play the flute."

I answer, "A lot of people happen to play the flute, but not everyone has the kind of character you do."

"Well," he responds, "it's been a wonderful ride, with some bumpy spots, but wonderful. You have to take the bumps and never say quit. If you get knocked down, get back up."

"Is there anything else that we haven't talked about that the readers of *The Flutist Quarterly* might want to know about your true self?"

"No, you've stuck the knife in all the spots I can think of." And then, Mark yet again launches into some of his professional adventures.

Oh, and the answer to my brilliant question? Red.

The Flutist Quarterly, Summer 2002

Göran Marcusson:
Dropping into a Dream

"It's just *disgusting* that anyone can play the flute that well," whispered my girlfriend between pieces as we attended a National Flute Association Convention concert, listening to Swedish flutist Göran Marcusson. We were mesmerized by his dazzling technique and gloriously singing tone; astounded by his impossibly soft pianissimos and the complete relaxation of his body. At a rest in the music, he hitched up his pants as casually as if he were in his own back yard. He made brilliant flute playing look as easy as tossing a ball. Definitely disgusting.

Many conventions later, at the recent one in Las Vegas, I invited Göran to tell me his story. I'd heard him perform several times in the interim, worn out his CDs, and added his name to my personal list of Favorite Flutists of the World. We sat in a quiet room at a small round table beside a window where the sun streamed in from a bright blue sky. Göran wore a black shirt with a mandarin collar and light khaki slacks, but what captivated me were his direct, intense blue eyes and his open, handsome face. I sat back, loving the Swedish accent in his near-perfect English, as he freely recounted his stunningly remarkable history.

"Yes, I will tell you my story—my flute story, and how I dropped into the business. And I will tell how I came to be here today, playing a concerto at the NFA convention.

"I was a flute owner from the age of 8. Because my mother played viola and cello and my father played organ and piano, there was always music at home. I wasn't particularly involved. I was into things kids are interested in, like sports and aircraft. I was determined to become a pilot. It was not just a kid's dream, because I had an uncle in the Air Force, and I built models and knew and read everything about aircraft.

"One day when I was skate sailing on the ice, I had a bad crash, and when my mother looked at my back she said 'Oh my god, your back looks like an *S*.' I was diagnosed with severe scoliosis and within half a year needed an operation. This would save my life but put an end to my dreams of being a pilot. I had to stay home for a year and could only go out under supervision. My grandmother and grandfather, a piano teacher, took care of me, and with him I began to play the flute a little every day. When you start to practice regularly at age 13 or 14, you develop so fast, and I began to like it. My passion became playing from my father's scores along with the records in his extensive collection. I thought it was so fun and I did it every day. I lost a year in school, but then I got a flute teacher and through him, I began to play in the local amateur orchestra. The first piece I played with them, as second flute, was Brahms' First, which I had played many times with the record. That was such a fantastic experience. Music became a new lifestyle for me.

"At 15 or 16, I auditioned for conservatory. Of course I wasn't good enough, but I was determined to become a musician. At 19 or 20, I lived a normal life as a student with all my friends, except that I practiced flute. I had never been to music school even though I continued to audition frequently.

"I didn't know what to do. Should I go into academics or what? I auditioned again but didn't get into any Swedish music school. I decided to give myself a last chance, so I *really* practiced hard for a year. I thought I'd get in with no problem, but again, I wasn't accepted. At that time I was really, really sad, depressed, crying, realizing I couldn't have my dream. When I look back, I can see why. They didn't know who I was. I had never attended a master class or taken a lesson from any of those guys on the jury.

"Meanwhile, to survive, I was working in a brick factory and started to drive a bus. I had passed my music history exam, but still I wasn't able to study the flute at a conservatory. At that time, I was actually encouraged by a teacher in Stockholm, from whom I took lessons, to choose another profession.

"Then, suddenly, I received a letter from the local tram company in Goteborg, the second largest city in Sweden, far from where I lived, saying that they were looking for a flute player for their wind band. The band members played two days a week and drove trams three days a week. I was standing there, thinking, 'This is it. Here is the crossroad.' I took the audition and got the job. So I started to drive a tram, and played a couple of days a week. I thought I'd give this a couple of years, and then *really* become a flute player even without an education; that I was going to make it *anyway*. After three years, though, I realized it would be impossible to get into the pro scene without having been in a conservatory.

"I took my first master class when I was about 22 to 23 with William Bennett and Trevor Wye at England's International Summer School at

Ramsgate. That was an eye-opener and changed my total approach. I partly realized why I hadn't gotten into school. I was wild. I had little understanding of style and phrasing. William Bennett, a fantastic teacher, talked every day about the French school, Moyse, Taffanel and Gaubert, how to treat music, phrasing techniques. I realized I had never done that.

"I decided to make one final audition when I was 24 to 25 years old. I only applied for the school in Goteborg because I had so many friends there and I didn't want to move. I was second on the waiting list, but very soon I was accepted. And suddenly I had a place.

"So that's when I started my music education. My advantage was that I had technique and tone even though they were undisciplined. And I'd been living with Jimmy Galway's recordings and I wanted to sound that way.

"After about a year and a half in school, a dispute occurred with a conductor who every student wanted to get fired. Because I was old (about seven years older than the others) and verbal, I was the one picked to carry the message to the board. So they said I was a troublemaker in the flute class. They offered me a position in another school just to get rid of me. I had to go down on my knees on the phone with my teacher and the office. I said I had to stay, that leaving was not an option, and I promised to be quiet, never open my mouth, and do my studies. My teacher accepted that, and then had to go on a long concert tour. In his absence we had some fantastic visiting teachers, like Robert Dick, Trevor Wye, and Jimmy Galway.

"At that time I took the initiative, on my own, to apply for the National Flute Association Young Artist Competition. That's one of the times when I've been so unbelievably lucky. I won the competition without knowing what the hell I was sticking my nose into. I had no clue what it was about. If I knew more about it, I probably would've been afraid to go. But it was 1987, and I wanted to see the world. I had to consult with Trevor Wye about how to make a program. He said, 'You start with something academic to present yourself as a musician. Then you play something beautiful to please them, and then you show off at the end.'

"My life changed completely from then on. Up to that point, I always had to struggle, to convince people, to prove myself. Here I got acknowledgment that I was good, that people liked what I was doing. Suddenly at home people looked at me differently; I got publicity, gigs, and subbed in orchestras. I began to take classes with Jimmy Galway in Dublin and Switzerland. His was the sound I was striving for, that singing sound that makes you so joyful. We became good friends, we played duets, and it was fantastic. The class had a scholarship which included a crystal flute from Waterford. Jimmy didn't want a competition so he left it to the students to decide, and they voted that I would get the scholarship and the flute. Jimmy came to Sweden and generously presented it to me on Swedish TV.

"I had better confidence, but even though I was old—in my 30s—I developed my flute playing through continuous practice. I knew so much about planning practice sessions and had a clear direction. I studied pieces very fast. Today, people don't always have a clear goal, how they want to sound, why they want to sound like that, why they play flute, what they want to do. Once they know that, it's easier to practice.

"Finally, I started to play concerts with the best ensembles in Sweden, and to play flute concertos, all the pieces I had always wanted to play.

"There are some problems in the music world. The people who judge auditions—they have an impossible job. I had such a strong desire to perform with my flute, I dare to say that nothing could stop me. If you can survive the problems, it makes you stronger. Today, I can't say it was bad. It made me the person I am. If a young person asks me what they should do, I never tell them to quit, even if it looks hopeless. Some adults come into classes relatively late in life, and I cannot say, 'don't do this.' They might have the same desire I had.

"I know from my own world, the satisfaction of doing this doesn't change whether you're doing it in Carnegie Hall or a local church. You have the same emotions going, it's just that you're doing it in different places. And if they're aware of this, then it's never too late. There's always a repertoire and opportunities and a place to play for everybody. And if you have an open mind when you go to a concert, you can hear a mediocre player but still receive the message and feel happy.

"I can tell you a good story about having a dream. I remember a 1983 James Bond movie called *Octopussy*. I bought the soundtrack and often listened to the fantastic alto flute playing while driving the tram, and I had a dream that maybe someday I would play this stuff, to be part of a motion picture. In the late '90s I lived in London. I was invited to a party at the home of the great English flute player, William Bennett, and across the table was flutist Adrian Brett. I had heard rumors that he was the one who had done this movie and so I asked him. 'Yes,' he said, 'it's me.' He told stories about how they recorded it. 'And you know that alto flute? I have it here. Do you want to try it?' And 15 years later I had come full circle, suddenly holding the instrument that produced those melodies. He said he didn't remember where the tune started or how it went. I said, 'Well, I do.' I remembered it started on a G, and I played it on that flute. And we had such a laugh, and I was so happy.

"One of the records I listened to when I was 17 was Stravinksy's *The Rite of Spring* with Michael Tilson Thomas conducting. Later, for a short time, I had the great privilege of playing first flute with the London Symphony Orchestra. The last concert before I moved back to Sweden included *The Rite of Spring* with Michael Tilson Thomas conducting. And that was also a moment of the greatest pleasure and satisfaction, an affirmation that there's hope on this planet, and that dreams can be fulfilled. I was doing in reality what I had dreamt about 20 years before.

"I don't know how the desire to play and the motivation to go to the practice room results in these dreams; I don't know how the road leads to them. The universe kind of curves into your life, and it happens. There is hope for everybody. The impossible can happen.

"I couldn't be where I am without the fantastic examples on recordings. But with recordings, we've lost an understanding of what the great composers did at their desks or pianos. When they wrote a piece out of their heads, only life—on rare occasions—could reproduce the piece. Everybody would listen. Today you have to push the music into people's ears. We've lost the listening. My wife and I threw out the TV six years ago."

I asked Göran whether he works to keep his body so relaxed. "Of course. You have to check on your body, make sure it's in balance. Work with your vibrato. It's impossible to make a good vibrato if you have tension in your chest, stomach, or throat. Once you know how you want your vibrato to sound, you must relax to achieve it; anything tense inside will stop you from making a good singing sound on the flute.

"Work with the tone as a voice, so it reflects emotions just like singers. We use the same muscles and expression as when we're laughing, crying, screaming. When vibrato is mechanical it is dead—it may give a color to the tone, but expressively it's dead. When vibrato transmits your inner emotions, like joy or despair, it's alive. When a person laughs, you hear if it's fake, or tense, or if it's a profound, happy laugh. When a person cries, you hear if it's desperate or if it's made up. You can hear nuances and levels.

"My goal is to open up those channels. I do my daily practice exercises adapted into Moyse or into scales so I can let out my inner feelings and relax. Check your body; there's always something going on: an arm is lifting, eyebrows are frowning, or the forehead is tense, so relax it. Move slightly when you are practicing. If you're a stick it's uncomfortable. Always work with your vibrato and move—but no big movements—and unlock what's inside."

Göran, 42, lives in the countryside outside of Goteborg in a remote place so small that "it's not even a village." His wife, Gitte, is a flute teacher, and they have a two-and-a-half-year-old daughter, Anne-Sofie, a newborn son, Kaspar, and two cats. Göran enjoys spending his free time gardening and cooking.

Göran Marcusson plays principal flute in the GoteborgsMusiken Wind Ensemble, which also serves as the Swedish Air Force Band. He teaches master classes and performs as soloist with orchestras around the world. Göran teaches at Wildacres Flute Retreat in North Carolina every June, and at the Newport Music Festival in Rhode Island each July. He has arranged and published a number of flute pieces and released seven solo recordings on the Intim Musik label and can be heard as soloist with many GoteborgsMusiken recordings on the Naxos label.

As we wound up our conversation, Göran said, "I have a true fascination for life. I think Bach is the greatest at being able to say that what we see in front of us is more than we human beings can believe. Such enormous feelings express what is beyond humanity. What's going on is unbelievable and it's *big*. When we think about it philosophically, not technically, it can't be put in words, but some composers can put it in music and tell us something about our existence.

"I'm very happy to realize I don't understand. I can form my life in a way that I dream of, and I am now picking the fruits of those dreams. My tool is my flute. Problems become so small. Experiences of life become big. If I smile at the world, the world smiles at me."

The Flutist Quarterly, Winter 2003

Tim Carey a.k.a. The Tim Philharmonic

The setting is a master class at Wildacres Flute Retreat. Flute instructors Bradley Garner and Göran Marcusson, and English pianist Tim Carey, decide to perform Doppler's "Andante and Rondo." They discover that they lack the piano part. "Oh, no problem," Tim says, waving his arm. "I'll make it up." So off they go, with Tim improvising a full accompaniment by listening to the two flute players. When the flutists stumble and get lost, Göran turns to Tim and asks, "Can we go back to 35?" knowing full well that Tim is playing without music—he has no measure 35. When a page of music drops from Brad's stand and they falter, Tim can't go on because he's literally following them by listening. Then, as soon as he hears where they are, they all continue. His barely-there smile shows us that he is in another world, enjoying every minute. Suddenly, he pretends he's having trouble turning pages which, of course, he doesn't have. Occasionally, he breaks into snatches of other recognizable classical pieces, or leans back in his chair popping one finger in his mouth. The trio, and those of us in class, are laughing and hooting so much we are barely able to sit in our chairs. If hilarity is good medicine, I'll be healthy for the next decade from this dose alone.

I've seen Tim rip into the piano with the jazziest of rhythms and, in the next moment, stun the audience with a brilliant rendition of a Rachmaninoff prelude. He can make an old upright sound like the Chicago Symphony for an intermediate student playing her first concerto, and I've heard him play a simple lullaby with the delicacy of a mother's gentle touch. Once you've heard him at the piano, you know his nickname is perfect: The Tim Philharmonic. The flute world is lucky, because this amazing musician spends 70 percent of his professional time collaborating with flutists.

Tim and I sat in rocking chairs on a shady porch at Wildacres Retreat in western North Carolina, looking at the sun shining on the magnificent Blue Ridge Mountains as we talked about his life.

"The flute stuff didn't begin until about 15 years ago," Tim said. "I started out concentrating on my solo career, but it didn't suit me. I enjoyed playing concertos with other people around, but I didn't like solo recitals. The first person who involved me in the flute business was the English flutist Clare Southworth. I played in her flute course, and there I met Göran, Liz Goodwin of Flutewise, and British flutists Ian Clarke and Mike Mower."

Tim toured with Mike Mower in England and abroad. They toured in Australia and attended the flute convention. Tim also played a recital with flutist Tadeu Coelho while they were there.

"I'd never heard fast tonguing like Tadeu's. Mike was turning pages for me and I asked him, 'You ever heard tonguing like that?' Mike said, 'That's proper tonguing, mate.' Just unbelievable. I've recorded all Mike's stuff with him and with others, but I'm not really a jazz pianist. I'd love to have been a jazz musician. I think the lifestyle would have suited me."

Tim has played with an impressive list of flute soloists, including Jonathan Snowden and Mike Cox, a principal in three London orchestras. Tim first came to the States with Göran. In 1997, he played in the Chicago National Flute Association Convention. He has toured with Teri Sundberg and Helen Blackburn, and has worked with Anna Thibeault, who is also course director of Wildacres Flute Retreat.

"I'd known Anna in England. She got me involved with the annual Wildacres Retreat, where I met Brad Garner. Wildacres has grown into a kind of family. We all look forward to seeing each other there. The quality of the music is almost as good as the pranks we play on each other. At other times during the year, I play for Ransom Wilson's courses and with Lisa Garner Santa. I learned a lot of the flute repertoire and know most of it now."

I asked Tim what is different about playing with flutists (or "flautists," as Tim calls us) compared to other musicians.

"There are so many fabulous women and not many blokes. Also, flautists are always late off tied notes. I always have to wait until they breathe," he quipped. "Another alarming thing about them," he said, laughing, "is that they never give you the music until the last minute."

I witnessed this myself at the British Flute Convention when one of the world's great piccolo players, Jean-Louis Beaumadier, announced from the stage halfway through the program that Tim was "not his regular pianist" but was substituting. Tim had just gotten the music the day before. "He sight-read all seven pieces perfectly, the first time through. We only had two rehearsals, and I told him about playing it with the French style. He had it perfectly at the recital." He shot the audience a thumbs-up. "A most fine pianist!"

In a more serious vein, Tim continued. "In an orchestra, I use my ears in many more different ways than when I play with one person. I'm more sensitive with a single player. And with a flautist, I often can't make a big sound as I can with a clarinet or violin player, whose instruments are more penetrating. I always worry when a flautist wants to play the *Franck Sonata* (in A Major) for example. Some have a big enough sound to do it, but some don't.

"The most important skill I have as an accompanist is to have fun with a person. If I can't get on with my musical partner, I won't be as obliging or as keen to communicate. I have to be willing to discuss the music and not be dogmatic—to engage in a healthy, friendly argument. Music is such a precarious business, and I've always been friendly and outgoing. I like to be everybody's friend. America is where I do my most enjoyable flute and piano stuff. I'm told that in this country, the English accent carries a lot of weight for making friends."

I caught Tim's eyes twinkling at this bit of silliness, so I told him it was time to take a picture. "Oh, Helen," he exclaimed in despair, "I need to do my hair. And I haven't cleaned my teeth! Should I look serious?" I told him he didn't have a serious bone in his body.

After photos, we turned to his interests outside of music. Tim speaks French, German, and Italian, plus a little Japanese and Swedish. He reads avidly and collects U.S. quarters. He thought he had them all until he discovered we have two different mints in the States, so now he's only halfway to completing his coin collection. Cars and airplanes are his abiding passions. He has owned 44 cars. As a child he made model aircraft, and when he grew up he got a pilot's license.

"Kitty Hawk is like a shrine that I've got to visit. It's a Mecca for people like me, to see where the Wright brothers flew their first plane. Life isn't just music and flute players. You have to get outside, get in touch with reality."

Reality interrupted us just then with the ringing of the Wildacres lunch bell. We sauntered to the light-filled cafeteria where Tim engaged in another of his favorite activities, eating, while I sought out his friends. I asked Brad Garner to tell me some stories about Tim.

"I couldn't tell you any that you could print," Brad responded, but he did tell me that Tim is one of the best master class pianists he's ever met. "He's so kind and supportive to the kids. With him at the piano, one cannot fail. He's always right there."

Göran Marcusson agreed. "Tim can get any nervous person to cool down. He'll tell just the right jokes at the right time. He'll drink spirits all night, sing like crazy and dance with everyone—absolutely everyone— and party until 5 A.M. But he'll be at the piano at 9 A.M. on the dot, ready for rehearsal. I'll get lost in a pedagogical jungle, but Tim will save the day when I get too philosophical."

After lunch, Tim and I perched ourselves back on the porch to enjoy the afternoon's tranquility while I asked about his childhood. Tim considers his roots to be in Somerset in the west of England, where he spent the first decade of his life.

"At age 6, I had already started piano lessons with a local teacher. We moved to Essex when I was 10, and I met the guy who taught me everything I know about the piano—an unknown man named Harold Parker. He devoted his life to the piano and he fired my enthusiasm. Harold was a unique figure. He was the major influence and inspiration in my life. He taught me how to move the fingers and thumbs, the history of piano performance, the mechanics, the repertoire, all of it. I came to trust him about everything.

"He was kindly but serious, and he could be sarcastic. One thing I didn't like was that he didn't let you play anything through. After two bars, it was stop. Stop. The next hour was spent talking about those two bars. He was exactly what I needed. I had loads of other interests—too many for my own good. But at age 13, piano playing took over. I just loved it. I don't remember deciding. It just happened.

"Later I had other teachers, including Louis Kentner, a well-known Hungarian musician whose brother-in-law was Yehudi Menuhin. He taught me about musical freedom. I also studied at the Royal College of Music for five years. I don't remember learning too much about piano playing, but I had a great time meeting people and playing chamber music.

"In my late 20s, I questioned everything, thinking perhaps I should restore cars instead of playing piano. But one day it became clear—like a sun flash—that this was not such a bad way to spend a life. Sometimes it's a bit difficult to see how to make a living, but I've gotten by," Tim laughed.

"I've always done a lot of private teaching and taught at the music college in Colchester. That was my main income at first, until I started to do more solo work. Later I had an ensemble, and I became the pianist for the Ulster Orchestra in Belfast.

"Although I can't make a sound on the flute, I must know more about the flute than many flautists! I love the subtlety of the flute. The National Flute Association convention, more than any other flute gathering, is a worldwide institution with a holiday feel. I love being part of that."

I asked Tim, "You sit there for hours at a time in master classes and look interested—do you get bored?"

"Sometimes," he admits. "The people are all different. If the teacher is someone like Göran, I'm there for the entertainment factor—never a dull moment. The variety comes from the different people playing. It doesn't matter if they're beginners or fantastic soloists, old or young. Everybody is unique. I get fed up with my own company rather quickly anyway, except at those times in life when you need to be by yourself.

"I've had black moments in my life, depression and that sort of thing. Relationship breakups have sparked off a chemical condition. Years ago, I had to see counselors and take pills. Those periods were very low, but they never got the better of me or lasted long. I was cured by a behavioral psychologist using cognitive therapy. I've always been a terrible worrier. Now I know how to talk to myself and put things in perspective. When I was young, I expected things to be perfect, but not anymore. I learned that everybody has problems even if they don't look like it. I accept it as part of being alive.

"I tend to live life to the fullest, so I'm not always in the best physical condition." Tim chuckled as he patted his midsection. "I have to pace myself a bit more these days. I'm 49 years old, and that's seriously old."

Tim may think he's seriously old, but his handsome looks can still increase the tempo of female hearts. He blushed when I suggested this, but I'm sure the woman in his life—his partner, Suzy—would agree. Although a marriage and previous relationships didn't succeed, Tim now shares a happy home in Chelmsford, England, with Suzy and their son, Louis, who is 4.

"I met Suzy, a freelance violinist, when we were touring in Milan with the Bournemouth Sinfonietta. We've been together 10 years. Our extended family includes Suzy's older son and my older children, who range in age from 10 to 20."

Tim and I began to reminisce about the first time we met at a 1996 Flutewise Convention in London. I thought Tim was the warmest, sweetest guy. I never thought I'd see him again, but he has visited me and my husband at our home in North Carolina on two occasions. He's become a dear, special friend.

Tim would love to come to America more often, he says. His goal is to expand his musical collaborations in the U.S. The flute community will be fortunate if he succeeds.

The last time Tim was in this country, he realized one of his dreams. He flew into Kitty Hawk, North Carolina, and walked along the flight path of the first powered flight. "It was marvelous," he said. "I thought, 'I made it here at last. Wow.'"

For us flutists, to play with The Tim Philharmonic is to live our sweetest musical dream—to make music with a pianist who understands our instrument, our music, and most importantly, us.

The Flutist Quarterly, Fall 2007

Tim has worked with a veritable Who's Who of distinguished flutists. Those cited in this story include:

Jean-Louis Beaumadier: International piccolo soloist, master teacher and recording artist.

Helen Blackburn: Principal flute, Dallas Opera Orchestra; flute instructor, Texas Christian University.

Ian Clarke: International flute soloist, master teacher, composer, film and television producer.

Tadeu Coehlo: International flute soloist, master clinician, recording artist and professor of flute, University of North Carolina School of the Arts.

Mike Cox: Co-principal flutist, BBC Symphony Orchestra; professor of flute, Royal Academy of Music.

Bradley Garner: Professor of flute, University of Cincinnati College-Conservatory of Music.

Lisa Garner Santa: Recording artist; professor of flute, Texas Tech University.

Liz Goodwin: Founder and Director of Flutewise; author of *The Fife Book*.

Mike Mower: Composer, flutist and saxophonist; owner of Itchy Fingers Publications.

Jonathan Snowden: Solo flutist and recording artist (film scores include *Lord of the Rings*).

Clare Southworth: Professor of flute, Royal Academy of Music.

Teri Sundberg: International performer; professor of flute, University of North Texas.

Anna Thibeault: Founder and Course Director of Wildacres Flute Retreat; flute instructor, Georgia Southern University.

Ransom Wilson: Conductor and professor of flute, Yale University.

The Balance is Heaven:

At Abbey Road Studios with Sir James Galway

OK, so, big deal. Jimmy is warming up for a gig, and I've heard him play thousands of times. Right now he and an engineer are discussing the quality of his tone as it's transmitted through tall, thin mics. Members of the orchestra drift toward their seats, instruments in backpacks, rolling carts, or under arms. Jimmy is handsome today, appears whole and healthy, dressed in a pink- and grey-striped shirt, rose tie, black vest and pants. His hair is slicked back, superstar-chic.

He's being photographed from all sides. Between shots, he plays snatches of flute pieces, orchestral excerpts, musical nonsense. The orchestra gets louder as they warm up. A big trolley rolls in with more instruments. A water bottle and two glasses are put on a table near Jimmy, who shimmers up and down scales, interrupting himself to talk to a violinist and show him a newspaper article.

Finally, the orchestra tunes. The conductor welcomes Jimmy, who in turn expresses his thanks for the enthusiasm. The rehearsal begins.

I'm an audience of one, perched on a comfortable couch just above and near Jimmy, observing him and the London Symphony Orchestra amid a mass of tangled mics, cables, and electronic paraphernalia inside historic Abbey Road Studios in London, where Sir James Galway is recording his next CD. This is a BIG deal, a singular, spectacular opportunity of a lifetime.

DAY ONE

Klauspeter Seibel, conductor of the Louisiana Philharmonic Orchestra, and Jimmy worked together two years ago. This is their first recording together.

CONDUCTOR: You're late on the downbeat, Jimmy. It's hard for us to wait. Can you come down with us?

JIMMY: Yes.

CONDUCTOR: How do you like the tempo?

JIMMY: It's a bit quick.

Studio One is massive, expansive enough to accommodate the large orchestra and more, with 60-foot ceilings and light blue acoustic walls. Jimmy wills his music to break through those walls, out to those waiting to hear his sweet sounds. He lifts his flute as he plays, transcending the studio's electronic limits to reach other realms.

ENGINEER: Watch the dynamics at measure 60.

So much for transcendence. I can tell they're beginning to record now, by watching the red recording lights go on and off on all four walls. I'm taking notes, but at one point the playing gets so heavenly, so tender, that I'm unable to hold my pen and notebook. I lay my head back and close my eyes.

At the end of the piece, Jimmy lets out a big "Whoo!" He's joined in similar sounds of relief from the orchestra and conductor. They'd played calmly but with an underlying awareness that a recording was being made.

ENGINEER: Let's check that.

Jimmy, the conductor, and the conductor's wife go into the control room. Jutta Seibel-Reumann is a lovely woman who was an opera singer. The orchestra members stand and stretch, sit around talking, tuning instruments until the rehearsal resumes.

CONDUCTOR (to the orchestra): Too much horn. I would like cleaner articulation, and you must follow Jimmy more.

All this time, Jimmy polishes the four Muramatsu flutes on the table beside him. He turns around and looks up at me with a big grin. When his flutes sparkle, he stands waiting patiently, hands clasped behind his back. I look carefully to make sure the red light is off, because I need to blow my nose. I blow while the conductor tunes two instruments. In that room, my nose sounds like an earthquake. Half the orchestra looks up at me and laughs. I smile back, wishing I had somewhere to hide.

JIMMY: Around measure 26, I split a note. And how's the intonation in there? This headjoint is a struggle, push in, push out.

More laughter.

CONDUCTOR: How's the balance?

PRODUCER: The balance is heaven.

Red light on, music starts. Music stops.

CONDUCTOR: Jimmy, you have four bars of rest before you come in.
JIMMY: Oh, I wasn't thinking. I was thinking of something else.

Red light on. Music starts. Jimmy messes up a note and stops playing. Music stops. Music starts. A violinist turns to the stand behind him and gives a woman a dirty look. Another violinist winks at her and she smiles. In the middle of the piece, the conductor stops.

CONDUCTOR: I heard something in the room.

Oh my God! I had just uncrossed my legs. I cringe sheepishly. Maybe they don't know it was me.

PRODUCER: Room noise. Go again.

During the break, I talk to Graham Chambers, librarian for the LSO. For 14 years he's been responsible for all the music the orchestra uses for concerts, films, everything. He procures it, organizes it, gets it ready for tours. He's gone on a hundred foreign tours and has seen the world, but he's had enough and stays home now.

He's taping photocopied music together as we converse. "Aren't you doing something illegal there?" I ask. He explains that if it comes from the copyright owner, it's okay. He tells me that no orchestral librarian ever uses scissors; with his teeth, he ferociously rips something he calls cellotape. In America we call that scotch tape, I tell him. "That's a silly name," he quips. "Where in America do you live?"

"North Carolina."

"Where's that?" he wants to know.

"North of South Carolina," I quip back.

He tells me the string parts he's taping together were received last night via email as PDF attachments and added to the sessions two days ago. The musicians sight-read everything.

The break is over. This time I sit in the control room, which is larger than I expected. The recording engineer is at the biggest mixing board I've ever seen, with screens above to allow a front view of the conductor. In one corner is the assistant engineer with two computer screens and another technical instrument. The producer is behind the engineer at his own table, with the assistant producer at her desk. In the back are sofas, where the executive producers from Deutsche Grammophon (DGG) sit, and a small table with water, fruit, and cookies. Two of the walls are full of computerized panels, unintelligible to me. Behind the control room is the machine room with more panels of lights, cables, electronics, computers, fail-safe technology; if the computer loses the audio files, they're preserved here.

PRODUCER: I wanted to record these two pieces first because the balance on these is the hardest.

JIMMY: May I have a little chair beside my music stand? (He's been standing for hours.) I bring my slippers to these things. They're falling apart, but they've been all over the world.

The producers, engineers, and executive producers are all following the score and, at times, they're all conducting, even though no one out in the room can see them. Their eyes burn, faces intense. Their bodies move with passion and involvement in the music.

The producer, Craig Leon, who has worked with Pavarotti, Sting, Joshua Bell, and others, marks his music in code about technical aspects. Cassell Webb, Craig's wife, is the assistant producer, an exotic-looking woman who sits near me and writes notes like, "Here is where he makes me weep."

Red light on, music starts.

PRODUCER: Low B is flat.

Music stops. Music starts again. Cell phone rings in orchestra. Music stops, everyone laughs. Music starts, Jimmy is still out of tune, but no one in the control room tells him. They say, can we have that passage again? Music starts. Doesn't work. Stop.

JIMMY: I have to look at the breathing. Sorry.

Red light on. Music starts. Stops and starts many times.

PRODUCER: Yes! He played the B in tune that time. Beautiful.

JIMMY: I was nervous. Sorry about that.

PRODUCER: We have ten minutes. I can do the rest of this piece in the next session. Let's go on to the next piece.

Lady Jeanne Galway enters and greets everyone warmly. She is relaxed and casual, in a tan sweater and ivory cotton slacks.

PRODUCER: Let's do this section once more for safety. We have to be running at 6:30 or we go into overtime. No talking. We can grab just that bar maybe tomorrow. Let's go to dinner.

I get my bag, and suddenly I'm alone in the studio. I don't know where everyone went to eat, so I go to the cafeteria down the hallway and find them there. In the food line, I speak to a second violinist who has been with the orchestra for 30 years. He tells me about the severe decrease in session work over the past few years. When I arrive at the end of the line, a man asks, "Is this on Studio One's account?"

I hesitate.

"I don't know," I answer, "but I'm a guest of James Galway's."

"I guess that counts," he says, and waves me by. I don't have to pay for my meal.

I eat partly with Jimmy, Craig, and Matthias Spindler, the DGG executive producer, and partly with Klauspeter and Jutta. I ask Craig to tell me what he feels is the most important job of a producer.

"To make the artist sound the best he can."

"Do you feel more anxious with someone you're producing for the first time, even after all your extensive experience?"

"No, I feel anxious no matter how many times I've worked with someone, because I want to do a good job."

I tell Klauspeter how kind and respectful a conductor he is.

"Why not? They're all nice people."

"Not all conductors are that way," I say.

He thanks me in his beautiful German accent. Jimmy tells me that he chose Klauspeter for this recording because while a lot of conductors know the tune, Klauspeter can read the score.

The next recording session is of Sir James and Lady Jeanne playing together. His stocky body sways in sync with her slender figure. Jimmy conducts to show her a tempo. The two flutes are lovely together. A violinist taps his toe in the air, making no noise.

Some of the orchestral musicians are dismissed. Earlier, I had tried to call my husband at a phone booth in the hallway. Jonathan Lipton, the longest serving fourth horn in the 100-year history of the LSO, assisted me. He's my age and grew up in New York City as I did. In the course of our conversation, we discovered that the next day is his 28th wedding anniversary and my 29th. I insist that he buy his wife a decent gift. As he leaves the studio, he mouths, "Happy Anniversary," and I return the wish.

Red light on, music starts.

Stop. Harp needs to re-tune. Music starts. Stops. Jimmy doesn't have the pages in the right order. Orchestra starts introduction. Jimmy is still polishing his flute, walks up to the music stand, comes in at the last second.

It's getting late. Matthias runs upstairs to fix parts on the Sibelius software for the two French horn players. He photocopies them and literally races back downstairs to give them to the musicians. Everything here is obviously well organized and has taken much preparation, but all the tools are available to make last-second changes if needed.

I look at the gift book I'd given Jimmy earlier in the day, Charles Snell's

*This is My Wish For You,** depicting a piccolo player on the last page, which I'd inscribed. He's kept it beside his flutes throughout this long day.

Red light on. Music starts. Jimmy cracks a note. Music stops.

JIMMY: If you want to start from the beginning, my lip will be on the floor. Take it from section C.

A violinist yawns. It's 11 P.M. Music starts. Music stops.

JIMMY: (Laughing) I used a wrong fingering.

PRODUCER: I'd like to do one more time between E and F. (They had done it dozens of times already.)

I see on the schedule we have only seven minutes left. The producer uses those minutes to start on tomorrow's first piece. Then everyone is dismissed. My friend Dara and her mother (the former Norma Evans who recorded a popular hit song in the 1950s in this very studio) pick me up.

DAY TWO

I arrive at 9:45 A.M. The orchestra is warming up. I don't see Jimmy, so I climb the steps to my perch. Halfway up, I hear an Irish whistle zipping through an amazing blur of notes. Instantly I turn to locate the whistler so I can give him a good-morning hug.

Cassell Webb greets me. She graciously makes sure my needs are taken care of, as well as keeping me out of everyone's way. I see Graham (the librarian) and tell him how excited I am. He says it's refreshing to have someone around for whom this is less humdrum than going to the bank. "Unless I have a check with lots of zeros in it," he adds.

A cameraman and sound guy are filming Jimmy today. They tell me they work for Universal Studios but are contracted to DGG for this job. The videos will be used as part of the EPKs (Electronic Press Kits) for interviews to send to markets for videos, or to acquire TV appearances for publicity.

The recording session begins. After a while, I go down to the machine room. I stick my head into the control room so I can hear the magnificent speakers. They're recording a piece newly composed for Jimmy, who's obviously refreshed this morning.

PRODUCER: Let's leave what's on here. I can't touch this. What am I doing here?

---

*C. Snell, *This is My Wish for You.* Seattle: Laughing Elephant Books, 1992.

ENGINEER: Can't mess with genius.

Jimmy passes by me as he walks to the control room and says, "Not bad for sight-reading, is it?"

The recording session goes on, with the producer asking for repeats because of someone playing on an open string (how did he hear that?), another musician coming in a little early, and the strings being too loud.

Jeannie arrives carrying her husband's lunch in a shopping bag. She says she hopes it'll stay warm until lunchtime.

I notice a quiet man standing in the machine room, arms crossed, carefully observing the session. I ask him who he is.

"Derek Bailey," the friendly man answers. "I'm from the same part of the world as Jimmy, his TV producer since 1975, including his first big documentary, his 50th birthday video, and other promotional films. Did you know," he asks, "that Jimmy's playing at a special concert in Belfast during the last night of the Proms this September? There'll be an audience of 6,000 outside the City Hall, and it'll be fed into the Proms* concert at Royal Albert Hall in London."

"Wow!"

The engineer asks the orchestra members to put on headsets. He sends them "clicks." A metronome is fed to everyone. Many tempo changes occur in the piece, and the beats need to be precise.

JIMMY: I don't like headphones. Apparently I'm not with the click.

Laughter everywhere.

Red light on. Music starts. Music stops.

PRODUCER: Something in the internal intonation in the strings is off. Ah, yes, that's better.

The role of the producer is underappreciated by the public. When I buy a CD, I know the label, of course, and I know the artist and conductor, who interpret and perform the music. The engineers technically capture the sounds. The executive producer has responsibility for what goes on the CD, discussing the repertoire with the artist, preparing the budget, hiring the orchestra, and more. But it's the producer who coordinates the whole recording, makes the music sound the way it does, helps the editor, allows the artist and orchestra to sound their best, keeps the flow and timing of the schedule, and works behind the scenes in countless ways.

Jeannie tells me that hardly anyone spends money to contract musi-

---

*The Proms is a London concert series sponsored by the BBC.

cians with major symphonies for CDs anymore, so this is a big deal, and it's with a major label, DGG, the best. It's not ordinary to have executive producers following scores the way these guys are doing here.

The repertoire on this CD has never been recorded by Jimmy before, I'm told, except for "Annie's Song,"* and all of it has been newly arranged for him by Craig Leon, the producer, except for "A Lord of the Rings Suite," which was done by Howard Shore.

I seek out Matthias Spindler of DGG and tell him how much flutists enjoy playing the music that Jimmy records, even feeling presumptuous enough to suggest publishing a book of these pieces. Of course, Matthias is already on top of the idea, but I figure flutists the world over will worship me forever for saying so.

CONDUCTOR: Jimmy, how far back would you like to start this?

JIMMY: (Cheerfully) Oh, at least as far back as the first disaster.

Red light on. Music starts. Music stops.

CONDUCTOR: Jimmy, you have the wrong notes.

Jimmy painstakingly changes his notes with a pencil, while the concertmaster helps him sound them out.

At the next break, I go to the orchestra and sit next to Moray Welsh, principal cello with the LSO for 10 years. He toured and made records with Jimmy from 1975–1985.

"I was young and lucky to play with Jimmy back then. I learned a lot from his vocal way of phrasing. We went to America and all over. When he became a superstar, it was a novel thing for someone like him to be a pop star as well. We had such a reception. The TV exposure created a scene that began a new era in those days. I still see him now and again, and have been to his house in Lucerne."

Back to more recording, more gorgeous music. It's 4:30 P.M., and I'm so mellow I lie lengthwise along the couch on my perch. The music washes over me like a massage of my body and soul.

JIMMY: Did you like that, Helen?

I tell him that I loved it.

JIMMY: It's a good piece to sleep to.

I realize with an inner grimace that Jimmy is good-naturedly telling me he knows I've been napping. I splash cold water on my face in the bathroom and go to the control room. Jimmy is saying that this piece

*"Annie's Song" was composed and recorded by John Denver.

doesn't work on flute. They decide to listen to the original guitar piece, and the assistant engineer pulls it up instantly.

JIMMY: Could we consider adding a harpsichord later?

PRODUCER: Yes, we could.

JIMMY: Let me try it on a tin whistle.

PRODUCER: (with Jimmy out of the room) He's a rare breed. He thinks of himself as an orchestral musician.

Jimmy plays on.

PRODUCER: We're left here with some time, but why use it if he's played like he has today?

The session is over. In two days, I haven't heard an angry or unkind word among all of the artistic personalities and technicians gathered to make the CD. I've seen Jimmy and the orchestra record takes of a composition so breathtakingly beautiful from start to finish that the red light never went off. I've also seen how everyone revered Jimmy's playing even though he stumbled.

I understand, at a deeper level now, why some of us have problems with perfectionism, thinking we need to sound like the greatest flutists on CDs. They all make mistakes, miscount, and have intonation problems, just like us. And put me, with my modest flute skills, into Abbey Road with that staff and equipment, and even I might sound pretty awesome . . . maybe.

It is 6:30 P.M. Jimmy, age 64, has been playing since 10 A.M. and spent his lunchtime giving an interview. At dismissal, he throws up his arms in gratitude. He cleans his flutes, then walks toward me, asking if I'd like to talk. We go to the cafeteria, where he orders a beer.

I eagerly ask Jimmy, "How are you different than you used to be?"

"When I got into religion, I wanted to express myself on higher terms. I've limited my circle of friends to three or four, and a lot of the ones I chopped haven't missed me. I can't support so many friendships. I don't go to the pub anymore. If I want to converse with a friend, I invite him to dinner. In the pub, you're everybody's property. My friendships have deepened, the kind you can rely on, the kind who'd help you in the middle of the night.

"I'm more influenced by Jesus Christ and His way of life than by the media. Lots of people look up to newspapers and TV and that becomes their God, but there are no moral principles there.

"Now I understand music better. I came from a background as poor as the young hero did in the book *Angela's Ashes*.* The music business is full of drinking and drugs. At some point you have to give your body and soul a rest."

"Observing you here, Jimmy, everything about you seems different," I offer. "Your body looked still and sedate while you waited endlessly. I saw you be patient, polite, and modest. You struck me as a true elder statesman of the flute, a grand and dignified gentleman." Jimmy was looking at me deeply, obviously pleased with my words but also a bit surprised.

I continued. "I hope you don't mind my saying so, but a lot of people, and I've seen it myself, have perceived you in master classes as impatient at times. Is that in the past now?"

Jimmy looked sheepish, but his voice sounded strong and sincere. "Yes, I was impatient. But it isn't my principle to be that way." I asked him how he's changed this trait.

"I've calmed down as I've gotten older. The change has happened very slowly. I started paying attention. Mostly I prayed, talked about it, and meditated. The other thing I did was strengthen my relationship with Jeannie. We've had a good marriage for 20 years. I hang with her now, instead of playing golf with the boys. We laugh, play flute, pray and eat, and spend every hour of the day together. A lot of couples don't truly communicate. They listen but don't communicate about family relationships, household matters, professional concerns, and leisure activities.

"We used to cook together, but now we have two cooks. We used to garden; now we have a gardener. Antonio drives me; he's my chauffeur. He's tremendous with plants, too. Our house is covered with orchids."

Jonathan Allen, the recording engineer, joins us at the table. He shares that he was a violinist majoring in musical theatre at London University. When he graduated, he wrote a letter to EMI Classics, which owns Abbey Road Studios, and learned everything about his profession here. As the senior engineer, it's his responsibility to make sure the music is being recorded smoothly and well. He uses the mixer to change the levels of the instruments. He tells me that the assistant engineer, Roland Heap, has a degree in sound engineering from Surrey University. It's his job to run the recording machine and get the music from the digital audio work stations into the computer. If the producer wants to go to take #120, it's his job to find that file. Jonathan specializes in classical and film music. When I ask him which project he has enjoyed the most, he answers, "The one that's coming up next."

*F. McCourt. *Angela's Ashes: A Memoir.* New York: Scribner, 1999.

The assistant producer comes by to get Jimmy. During our talk, the editor was in the control room with the engineers and producers, editing a piece needed by someone the next day. Jimmy has to approve the finished product, not polished to perfection for the CD, but enough for the film. I go along and hear, somehow created from all the starts and stops of the last two days, the most soaring music, the strings glorious, the flute phenomenal. The track is a masterpiece of monumental proportions. The first edit of the three tracks will be completed by tomorrow night, and after two more edits, the final edit will be ready for Jimmy's approval in three weeks. The CD will be released in September 2004.

I thank Jimmy and hug him goodbye. "Hey, we're going to vacation in the Caribbean," he informs me, "but I won't be getting sand in my toes. I never stop playing the flute. I do it real well."

I smile and sneak in one last question. I want to know how Jimmy's religious beliefs connect to his music. He says, "I take a moment to ask my Creator to inspire me to play well. I need all the help I can get. I have this gift, and it would be wrong to ignore it, just as it would be wrong if I ignored any other kind of gift someone brought me. I'm grateful to have it, because maybe He meant it for the kid next door."

The Flutist Quarterly, Fall 2004

And the Surprises Keep Coming ...

As I finished editing this collection of essays on my life in music, I realized that I had begun another chapter in my career and there was one more story to tell. So, on Thanksgiving Day, appropriately enough, I composed this last essay on my new mission—working with musicians and others struggling to overcome performance anxiety.

Francene was the principal flutist in a highly regarded symphony orchestra on the West Coast. Two weeks prior to the opening of their rehearsal season, she sent me an email that was a poignant cry for help.

"While I have always had performance anxiety, I seem to be getting worse. With the beginning of our season only two weeks away, my anxiety is almost debilitating, and I am almost at the point of leaving the orchestra if things do not improve. I desperately would like to find some joy in playing again."

Francene is not alone.* I've known so many musicians—including my younger self—who suffer from fears that cripple performance and steal the ability to perform with joy, competency and freedom.

I was able to help Francene thanks to another one of life's surprises— the discovery of my second music-inspired career as a performance anxiety coach. I found my new mission quite by accident in 2001 in the beautiful North Carolina mountains at Wildacres Flute Retreat. I had received an invitation from director Anna Thibeault to be a guest at Wildacres where students, adult amateurs, and professional flutists gather each summer with master teachers for a week of classes and concerts. In return for this gracious gift, I offered to teach a class and sent Anna a list of eight topics I could discuss. She chose "performance anxiety."

This is a topic particularly close to my heart. Like every music teacher,

---

*Francene and Soledad (introduced later in the story) are not my clients' real names; I have changed their names to protect their privacy.

I had encountered performance anxiety in my students. As I encouraged them to get on stage and share the music they'd worked so hard on, I knew how they felt. Deep inside me, I could feel their dread—the uncontrollable physical symptoms, the humiliation.

I had overcome severe, crippling performance nerves in myself, as both a musical performer and a public speaker. I remember my first case of nerves in the fourth grade, when I had to make a presentation to my class and my arms shook horribly as I attempted to hold a piece of equipment that I was describing. By the time I got to college, I couldn't raise my hand in class to ask or answer a question. As a flutist, I happily played in orchestras, but I avoided recitals because I felt I wasn't as good a musician as everyone else and my listeners would think poorly of me. My body shook uncontrollably and I was unable to play in recitals with the musical expressiveness that I could feel in my heart.

It wasn't until my early 30s that I began to explore why I was so intimidated in front of others. I learned that my performance anxiety had a great deal to do with how I was raised. I had developed a low sense of my own worth and an excessive need for others' approval. When I learned to put those things in perspective, I began to be able to perform with confidence, but it took me many years of painful struggle to do so. I now love to be in front of an audience, and I am never afraid. But I can still remember how the terror stopped me from playing as beautifully as I knew I could.

So at that first class at Wildacres, I listened to the stories of the 20 or so teens, adults, and retirees sitting around the fireplace, and I openly shared my own. I told them that most people don't need to struggle as long as I did to find the ability to perform on stage at their best, because now we understand how to use effective techniques—like positive self-talk, relaxation, and mental visualization—that can help performers master their fears, often in a short time.

My one-hour Wildacres class stretched into two hours, because the students wouldn't leave. I learned that after the session, they found Anna, exclaiming, "You *must* have this class again next year." So the following year and every year since, I have returned as a faculty member to teach a one-week class called "Perform Confidently from Inside Out."

To teach that first class, I spent a year reading and studying everything I could about performance anxiety. I took online classes about the latest brain research related to performance. And as I worked with students, I realized that the national certification I had earned years earlier in grief counseling had taught me to listen deeply, to get myself out of the way, to encourage without demanding, and to support while allowing the other person to do the work.

Word began to spread about the Wildacres course, and I began receiving invitations to present workshops at flute festivals, universities, and private studios. My inbox began to fill with emails from performance artists who wanted to gain more control on stage. And I came to realize the profound and pervasive need—among professionals, amateurs, and students alike—to understand performance anxiety and to overcome the pain and frustration it causes throughout the music field.

My work with people like Francene taught me how individual each person's story is, yet how common the issues are. There was the student who felt he had to be perfect in order to make it in the music world. With guidance he learned to be more compassionate toward himself. There was the seasoned orchestra player who felt trapped by her reliance on beta blockers. She now uses her mind to help her relax instead of drugs. There was the 60-year-old amateur who hadn't played music for 40 years for fear of falling apart in front of others. She now plays regularly in church and at nursing homes.

For Francene, the healing began as she discovered how negative her thoughts were. She perceived the orchestra as a hostile environment where everyone criticized her every note.

"I have to fight, I have to survive, because I'm not really good enough to be here," she confessed. "Everyone else went to better schools and they're better musicians, even though I've earned tenure. This is too hard. I can't do it."

Francene learned to change these thoughts to positive self-talk statements and practiced using her positive thoughts to calm herself, regain her confidence, and see things in their proper, realistic perspective. In two weeks, she was ready to go back to work, although she was still very nervous.

It took time, but gradually Francene came to believe that she deserves to be in the orchestra. Now she reminds herself of this regularly, in ways that are meaningful to her. She learned to treat herself with much greater compassion and empowered herself to feel safe and confident as an orchestra member. It took weekly sessions and hard work to put her positive self-talk and relaxation skills into practice. A year later, just prior to the new orchestra season, she said: "I feel calm and ready. I'm actually looking forward to our first rehearsal, with no dread or panic. I cannot believe how far I've come this year as a person and a performer."

I soon found myself working not only with flutists like Francene but with other instrumentalists and singers as well as public speakers, actors, and dancers. One was Soledad, a busy mother of two teens who was a beautiful, accomplished ballerina. An unpaid amateur, Soledad danced for the love of her art. She sent me some videos of her performances—her dancing was gorgeous! But her fear of performance was close to destroying her joy in dance.

"I always get stupid nervous to the point where I wished I would never do this again," Soledad told me. In our first session, she talked about her belief that she had to be perfect and about how, on performance days, she would be curled up on her couch, incapable of functioning. When it was time for her entrance, her body would shake fiercely as she waited in the wings for her cue.

Soledad learned to mentally visualize dancing for herself with joy, releasing the need for others' approval, and having fun. She learned to keep high standards for her art, but not to strive for unreasonable perfection. We had only worked together in three sessions when she had a solo performance. Afterwards, I received an email from her:

"The most amazing thing happened. I did my visualizations every day. And opening night came. And ohmygawd Helen—I was steady in the wings. I danced only for myself. No terror, no out of control trembling, and I was present in the moment. And most amazing of all—I had fuuuuun!!! Wow. Thank you."

That's exactly how I felt—wow!—reading about Soledad's victory. I was right there with her, feeling triumphant about her profound breakthrough. Soledad was amazed that she could dance joyously. And I'm just as surprised that I—who was so intimidated in college that I couldn't raise my hand in class, who was too afraid to play my flute as a soloist—can teach people to perform confidently.

For 23 years I loved teaching children and adults to play flute, to make music and experience that joy in their lives. Now I teach people to express themselves with freedom and confidence, to give their gifts to others, and to perform with concentration and control even when the stakes are high. In victories like Soledad's and Francene's, I've found a new dimension of service to my fellow musicians.

How amazing! I don't have a degree in music, and yet here I am helping professors in music conservatories and coaching countless musicians to win competitions, gain entrance to graduate programs, and attain orchestra positions. And I find just as much joy and satisfaction helping the amateur flutist whose greatest desire is to play in church but who quakes in fear at the thought. I thrill to hear about her first exciting, joyous Sunday morning performance.

I am deeply grateful that I have been able to follow my heart where it led me, and to encourage others to do the same. It is our hearts that bring us to the wholeness of our great potential, to the satisfaction of living life to its fullest with joy abounding.

Thanksgiving Day, 2011
Chapel Hill, North Carolina

Acknowledgments

As I sit down to express my thanks to everyone who brought this book to life, my heart overflows with gratitude for the goodness, kindness, generosity, and love in the people who surround me daily.

Sometimes people are put in each other's lives to be angels to each other, and that is how I feel about my editor, Mara Gabriel. Mara first walked into my life as an adult flute student. We became close friends, and because she is a writer by profession, I asked her to edit my book. She shaped my huge pile of articles and crafted them into a cohesive narrative. Every nook and cranny of this book has on it her brilliant mark, her humorous smile, and her deep understanding of my intent. I am deeply and forever grateful for her dedication, elegance, and wisdom. This book would not be what it is without Mara's loving attention.

A. J. Mayhew, through her editing of my early articles, taught me how to write. Back in the days when editing was done with pen and paper, she took the time explain *why* she changed my words or phrases. When I was offered a column after writing only my second article, I asked her, "How can I possibly come up with something to write every other month?" She encouraged me enthusiastically and kept pushing me to become a better writer.

Salutations are due to my magazine editors over the years: Ted Rust of *Music for the Love of It* for publishing my first article and offering me a column after the second, Mary O'Brien of *Flute Focus*, Mary Jean Simpson and Anne Welsbacher of *The Flutist Quarterly*, Robert Bigio of *Pan*, now *Flute Magazine*, Victoria Jicha of *Flute Talk*, and Rosene Rohrer of the Raleigh Area Flute Association's *Tune In*.

Many thanks to Tod Brody, Dorrie Casey, John Wion, Jean Wright, and Joan Strauss for reading the manuscript and giving me feedback from musicians' and non-musicians' viewpoints. It was my Aunt Joan, a writer of children's stories, who first told me that I had a writer's voice in these articles—before I even knew what that was. Wissam Boustany, Tadeu Coelho, Brooks de Wetter-Smith, Daniel Dorff, Jill Felber, Ruth Sieber Johnson, Gerald Klickstein, Rhonda Larson, Lowell Liebermann, and Alexa Still kindly read the manuscript with great enthusiasm. I am also grateful to Nathan Zalman, fellow flutist, fellow writer, and dear friend, for consulting with me regarding technical aspects of publishing this book. I am indebted to the knowledgeable Carolyn Nussbaum of Carolyn Nussbaum Music Company for the time she took to impart excellent business advice regarding the selling of books. Adam Kissel showed impeccable professionalism and vast patience as he proofread and handled issues regarding the final manuscript. I appreciate deeply the vast experience and wisdom that David Perry and Heidi Perov of the University of North Carolina Press shared with me about book production. The wonderfully creative team at BW&A Books, Inc., especially Barbara Williams and Julie Allred, designed the cover, coordinated the production and printing, and made this book beautiful. My friend Bev Dwane of Bev Dwane Image Consulting offered helpful input regarding the cover colors. And many thanks to Amanda Allen and Robin Burk for their editorial help, assistance that gave me time to devote to my writing and editing.

This list of gratitutions, to use a word from the musical play *Wicked*, would not be complete without a major "hats off" to FLUTE List, the Internet discussion group of which I have been a member since its inception in 1996. Managed by Larry Krantz, Nelson Pardee, and John Rayworth—all precious friends—FLUTE List opened new worlds of communication and connection for me.

Although I am one person, based in my home and studio in Chapel Hill, North Carolina, I feel a profound connection to literally thousands of people in the flute community—performers, teachers, students, composers, flute makers, and sellers. I see these friends and colleagues at flute conventions, performances, and workshops. We visit on our travels and stay in touch on the Internet. I am in love with this community and with the feeling of belonging to it. It would be impossible to list them all, but their energy, their dedication to music, and their gift of surrounding me with a vast array of diversity, knowledge, skill, and courage has informed the making of this book. My heartfelt thanks go to each of you. And special thanks to everyone who gave me permission to include your personal and public communications in this book.

My stories are woven from a lifetime of experiences with my students and teachers. I am deeply appreciative to my flute teachers: Mr. Rabin;

Mr. Henry Zlotnik, who played with Phillip Sousa's band; Dr. Ronald Waln; and especially Dr. Brooks de Wetter-Smith, with whom I studied as an adult for 12 years. He taught me to make music rather than merely play the flute, and he opened my ears and expanded my consciousness to a universe of flutists worldwide. I will always remember the conductors of all the orchestras under whose batons I played and experienced the grandeur of symphonic music. Their teachings are still deep in my bones.

Every teacher of worth is taught by her own students, and I am humbled by the deep learning, joy, and love that my students have extended to me, from the youngest at age 5 to the oldest at age 70. Many still keep in touch, and I wish to acknowledge several who continue to share their lives with me as young adults: Martha Long, who is Principal Flute of the San Antonio Symphony Orchestra; Adam Cutchin, who is pursuing a PhD in French Literature; Alexandra Swanson, who is headed to Korea for a year prior to attending graduate school; and Janette Fant and Carly Yusiewicz, who are nurses. I am so proud of you—you make my heart sing! And to my adult students, an enormous thank you for your wondrous presence in my life. Walking with you through musical and personal struggles and triumphs has been an honor and a privilege. I have become a better teacher, musician, and person through our precious time together.

I am grateful for my nearly 20-year association with Unity Center of Peace, Chapel Hill, where I learned to become a confident performer, where the people encouraged me, and where I immersed myself as Music Director for more than 11 years. I can never thank Julie Harris enough for her many hours at the piano, for her patience and dedication to excellent and expressive music making, and for her loving attention to accompanying my students at their recitals.

My own musical journey began as I was growing up in the tiny New York City apartment of my parents, Lore and Richard Berger, who immigrated to the United States without a penny and unable to speak English. I am forever grateful for the classical music my parents played on the radio all day long, for the money they always managed to find to provide me with flute lessons, and for the support they gave me by faithfully attending all of my orchestra concerts.

I shared those early days in music with my friend, Toni Cogen Kerble. Toni and I lived on the same block growing up. As young teens, we spent Saturdays together in orchestra rehearsals. Eight hours of rehearsal was never enough, so afterward, we played duets in her parents' car. I'm so happy that she searched for me for 20 years until she finally found me again. Many more friends have enriched my life over the years. Hugs and love to my insightful confidantes Sigrun Bynum and Lea Pearson, my devoted prayer partner Karen Bogardus, and my beloved South African cousin Lisle Mayer. They have been with me through thick and thin and have enthusiastically supported my many projects.

The biggest miracle of my life is the daughter of my heart, Amy Lewis, whom I have loved since she was 3 years old. Amy and her husband, Tommy, and their children, Carlee and Keaton—my grandchildren, who call me Nana—are my beloved family. Without them, I would have a wonderful life in soft pastels; because of them, I have a glowing, vivid life in brilliant color.

Without my husband Fred, to whom I've been married for 37 years, I would not have a life in music at all. Because of his love, his generous spirit, and the long hours of hard work he devotes to his own profession, I have been able to pursue a career that brings me joy rather than one that just puts groceries in the cupboard. Freddy has lived every experience with me. He has been the steadfast friend beside me, holding me when I'm weak, whispering in my ear the happy and sometimes not-so-happy truths that I need to hear. Freddy has been my mate since I was 16 years old, and my love for him is boundless. He deserves, and has, my most profound gratitude of all.

Love, *Helen*

Bibliography

Bowen, Catherine Drinker. *Friends and Fiddlers*. Boston: Little Brown, 1942, p. 8.

Chase, M. P. *Just Being at the Piano*. Berkeley: Creative Arts Book Co., 1985, p. 7.

Johnson, G. W. *A Little Night-Music: Discoveries in the Exploitation of an Art*. New York: Harper and Brothers, 1937, pp. 124–125.

Judy, Stephanie. *Making Music for the Joy of It: Enhancing Creativity, Skills, and Musical Confidence*. Los Angeles: Tarcher, 1990, pp. xi, 31, 32, 69.

Lozoff, B. *We're All Doing Time*. Hanuman Foundation, 1978, in the newsletter "A Little Good News."

Mathieu, W. A. *The Listening Book: Discovering Your Own Music*. Boston: Shambhala, 1991, pp. 83, 101, 113, 116, 118, 119, 120, 123, 124.

Mathieu, W. A. *The Musical Life: Reflections on What It Is and How to Live It*. Boston: Shambhala, 1994, pp. xi, 150.

Sudo, P. *Zen Guitar*. New York: Simon and Schuster, 1998, p. 100.

About the Author

Flutist, teacher, and performance anxiety coach Helen Spielman lives in Chapel Hill, North Carolina.

She is a Distinguished Honorary Member of Sigma Alpha Iota International Music Fraternity and a Fulbright Senior Specialist. Helen loves reading, arranging flowers, and hiking. She has been married to her beloved husband, Fred, for 38 years, with whom she loves to travel the inner and outer worlds.

Please visit Helen's website, PerformConfidently.com, if you would like information about her workshops or about scheduling a confidential lesson regarding performance anxiety. Helen will also be happy to hear from readers who would like to comment on *A Flute in My Refrigerator*. Her email address is Helen@PerformConfidently.com.

Made in the USA
Charleston, SC
12 June 2013